W9-AZD-871

PRESENTED BY

Pat Engel
in honor of
Jean Bynum

CULTURES OF THE WORLD®

GREECE

Jill Dubois/Xenia Skoura/Olga Gratsaniti

BENCHMARK BOOKS

MARSHALL CAVENDISH
NEW YORK

PICTURE CREDITS
Cover photo: © Loukas Hapsis/On Location
AFP: 43, 45, 51, 53, 112, 114, 115, 117, 118 • APA Photo Agency: 61, 121 • Art Directors & Trip: 14, 38, 64, 69, 70, 73, 79, 80, 81, 106, 110, 119, 124, 131 • Bes Stock: 98 (right) • Jan Butchofsky/Houserstock: 30, 98 (left), 98 (center) • Camera Press: 29, 33 • Bira Da Silveira: 97 • Focus Team: 12, 20, 62, 108, 127, 130 • Getty Images/Hulton Archive: 27, 28, 49, 52, 95, 96, 104, 111 • Greek National Tourist Office: 26, 37, 65, 116, 120 • Haga Library: 36, 54 • Sonia Halliday Photographs: 22 • Dave G. Houser/Houserstock: 7, 58, 105 • International Photobank: 5 • John R. Jones: 1, 6, 9, 15, 16, 19, 24, 34, 42, 55, 76, 78, 84, 92, 93, 99 • Andre Laubier: 32, 40, 75, 82 • Les Voyageurs: 18, 102 • Life File Photographic Library: 10, 11, 13, 17, 21, 25, 44, 59, 66, 113 • Lonely Planet Images: 41, 46, 47, 48, 50, 57, 60, 68, 71, 72, 74, 85, 86, 87, 89, 107, 109, 122, 123, 125, 126, 128 • MacQuitty International Collection: 39 • Raymond Ng: 3, 4, 83 • North Wind Picture Archives: 103 • Olympic Airways: 129 • David Simson: 8, 56 • Topham Picturepoint: 67, 101

ACKNOWLEDGMENTS
With thanks to Eleni N. Gage for her expert reading of this manuscript

PRECEDING PAGE
Two young village girls from Karpathos, in the Dodecanese islands, wear dazzling costumes decorated with golden coins during the Feast of the Assumption.

Marshall Cavendish Corporation
99 White Plains Road
Tarrytown, NY 10591
Website: www.marshallcavendish.com

© 1992, 2003 by Times Media Private Limited
All rights reserved. First edition 1992. Second edition 2003.

Originated and designed by
Times Books International, an imprint of
Times Media Private Limited, a member of
Times International Publishing

Printed in Malaysia

Library of Congress Cataloging-in-Publication Data
DuBois, Jill, 1952–
    Greece / by Jill Dubois, Xenia Skoura, and Olga Gratsaniti.—2nd ed.
        p. cm.—(Cultures of the world)
    Summary: Introduces the geography, history, economics, culture, and people of the Mediterranean country of Greece.
    Includes bibliographical references and index.
    ISBN 0-7614-1499-1
    1. Greece—Juvenile literature. [1. Greece.] I. Skoura, Xenia. II. Gratsaniti, Olga.
III. Title. IV. Series: Cultures of the world (2nd ed.)
DF717.D832 2003
949.5—dc21   2002011625

7 6 5 4 3

CONTENTS

White houses and narrow roads cover an entire hill in the island of Santorini.

**The blue dome of a church
stands out among the
rugged cliffs of Santorini.**

INTRODUCTION

THE GOLDEN AGE OF GREEK CIVILIZATION more than 2,000 years ago laid the foundation for European philosophy and science, created beautiful art and architecture, and developed an intellectual and political life that has influenced the rest of the world for centuries.

Yet, despite their illustrious history, the people of Greece are now striving to gain a role in world affairs. Although the birthplace of democracy, Greece endured political and cultural oppression for centuries. Still, the Greeks' deep sense of cultural unity has preserved this rich society through occupation, wars, and political strife. In the last 40 years Greece has grown from a mainly agricultural country into a modern society thanks to the perseverance of its people.

A member of the European Union, Greece is located on the southernmost part of the Balkan Peninsula on the shores of the Mediterranean Sea. This central location, not far from Asia and Africa, has made Greece, historically, a "crossroad of cultures."

GEOGRAPHY

GREECE LIES AT THE CROSSROADS of three continents. The country is located at the southeastern corner of Europe on the southern part of the Balkan Peninsula. Continental Asia lies to the east of Greece, and Africa lies south across the Mediterranean Sea.

Greece is nearly surrounded by water. The farthest inland point in Greece is only about 50 miles (80.5 km) from the sea. The country is bordered by the Aegean Sea on the east, the Mediterranean Sea on the south, and the Ionian Sea on the west. In the north, Greece shares a boundary with Albania, the former Yugoslav republic of Macedonia, and Bulgaria. Its neighbor in the northeast and across the Aegean Sea is Turkey.

With an area of 50,949 square miles (131,958 square km), Greece is about the same size as England or the state of Alabama. About one-fifth of the total Greek land area consists of 2,600 islands scattered across the country's surrounding seas. About 1,200 of these islands are inhabited, while others are merely rocky outcrops. Greece is famous for its jagged coastline, which totals about 8,498 miles (13,676 km) in length.

Left: **Wildflowers bloom on the hills of the village of Dryopsis.**

Opposite: **Numerous islands form part of Greece. The beautiful Gialos harbor is located in Symi, one of the Dodecanese islands.**

LAND OF MOUNTAINS

The mountain ranges of Greece have served as a natural barrier against foreign invasion. They have also limited the amount of land available for farming.

Greece is a mountainous country. Rugged mountains cover three-fourths of the Greek mainland. The Pindus mountain range runs from Albania and the former Yugoslav republic of Macedonia in the north, through northeastern and central Greece and on to the Peloponnese in the south.

The areas lying between the mountain ranges form the Greek lowlands, which account for just 20 percent of Greek territory. The lowlands consist of flat plains located mainly along the coast, between the mountains and the sea. Other lowlands include mountain basins and valleys that have been cultivated, and flat lands near river deltas.

Mainland Greece is divided into seven regions: Macedonia, Thrace, Epirus, Thessaly, Central Greece (also called Sterea Ellas), Attica, and the Peloponnese.

Epirus, on the northwestern corner of the Greek peninsula bordering Albania, is the most mountainous region. Thessaly, however, is home to the highest mountain in Greece, Mount Olympus. Prominent in ancient Greek literature and mythology, it rises to 9,567 feet (2,917 m).

The Peloponnese is actually a large peninsula, joined to the rest of mainland Greece by a narrow strip of land called the Isthmus of Corinth. The Corinth Canal, originally commissioned by the Roman emperor Nero in the fifth century B.C., was only completed at the end of the 19th century.

The Greek islands are spread across the Ionian and Aegean seas. Crete, Greece's largest island, has an area of 3,218 square miles (8,335 square km) and lies in the Mediterranean at the entrance to the Aegean Sea.

The Ionian islands include Corfu, Leukás, Cephalonia, Zákinthos (Zante), Ithaka, Paxos, Kythera, and smaller satellite islands.

The Aegean islands are more numerous—they include Samothrace, Lemnos, and Lésbos in the north; the Sporades in the west; the Cyclades in the center; and Sámos, Rhodes, and the Dodecanese islands in the southeast.

Many of the islands are also mountainous; for instance, the mountains of Crete are part of the Pindus mountain range. Santorini (Thíra) was nearly destroyed by volcanic eruptions around 1500 B.C.

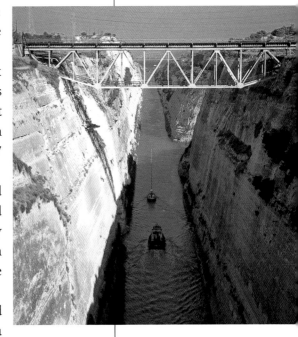

Above: **The Corinth Canal allows the passage of ships from the Mediterranean Sea to the Aegean Sea.**

Opposite: **The Voidomatis River valley in northwestern Greece.**

Red geraniums thrive in the sunny Mediterranean weather of Greece.

RIVERS AND LAKES

Greece has few rivers and lakes. None of the rivers are navigable because of the mountainous terrain, so they are not used for transporting people or goods. Many of the smaller rivers even dry up in the summer. The most important rivers in Greece include the Achelous, Peneus, Axiós, and Struma.

The country's largest lakes are located in the northern region. They include Ioánnina, Kastoria, and Prespa.

FLORA AND FAUNA

Many flowers, shrubs, and trees can be found throughout Greece including tulips, laurel, acacia, bougainvillea, hibiscus, jasmine, mimosa, oleander, and sycamore. Greece has about 6,000 species of wildflowers. Anemone, poppies, and cyclamen are found in areas over 4,000 feet (1,219 m), while mosses and lichen grow in regions above 5,000 feet (1,523 m). Plants that tolerate Greece's stony soil include thyme, bellflowers, grape hyacinth, star of Bethlehem, and yarrow.

About 20 percent of Greece is covered in forest. In the north and at higher altitudes, coniferous forests of Grecian fir and black pine thrive. Deciduous trees such as oak and chestnut grow at lower altitudes. Pines, planes, and poplars also thrive along Greece's rocky slopes and coastal plains.

Among the wildlife found in the forested regions, especially in the north, are the brown bear, wildcat, chamois (a goatlike antelope), deer, fox, badger, and weasel. Wolves and lynx are becoming rare. Farther

The *agriokatsiko* ("ahg-ree-oh-KAHT-see-koh"), or wild goat of Greece, makes its home in rocky, mountainous regions.

south, jackals, foxes, wild goats, and porcupines are found.

Many birds from northern and central Europe migrate to Greece for the winter. Among the birds of Greece are the hawk, eagle, egret, nightingale, partridge, pheasant, pelican, stork, and turtledove.

One of Greece's most interesting creatures is found in the sea: a shellfish called murex, which was used thousands of years ago to produce a purple dye for coloring the clothing of wealthy people. Other marine creatures include octopuses, which live along the shore, hiding behind rocks to protect their soft bodies from marine predators. Octopuses range in size from very tiny to more than 14 feet (4.3 m) across. Even larger are the squid, which can grow as long as 75 feet (23 m). Other common animals found in the warm waters of the Mediterranean are dolphins, seals, and turtles. Some species of sea turtles are in danger of extinction.

The modern city of Athens is a bustling metropolis.

CITIES

Over 40 percent of the population lives in the capital, Athens (called Athina in Greek). Overall, about two-thirds of contemporary Greeks live in urban areas. Although small in comparison to the Greek capital, other urban centers such as Thessaloníki, Patras, Volos, Larissa, and Iráklion (Heraklion) on the island of Crete, have grown rapidly since the 1990s.

ATHENS Athens is the political and commercial hub of Greece. It lies in a valley between three mountains—Pendelikón, Hymettus, and Parnitha. The city is centered on two hills—the Acropolis and Lycabettus.

Although Athens was the center of Greek civilization for more than 5,000 years, it has been the capital of Greece only since 1834.

During the Turkish occupation of Greece from 1453 to 1812, Athens declined in importance as Constantinople (now Istanbul, a city in Turkey) attracted more trade. By the time Greece gained independence in 1821, Athens had been reduced to a sprawling village. Since becoming the capital of independent Greece, the population of Athens has risen from 10,000 in 1834 to 3.6 million in 2001.

The city of Athens has grown so much since the end of World War II that its traditional boundaries have been stretched to the port of Piraeus, 6 miles (9.7 km) from the city center. One of the largest ports in the Mediterranean, Piraeus has a population of 880,000 and is home to Greece's merchant navy, one of the largest in the world. More than half of Greece's manufacturing industry is located here. Piraeus is a vital industrial area, with hundreds of factories producing tobacco products, fertilizers, cloth, and chemicals.

Rapid growth in the capital, however, has produced urban problems. Poor city planning has resulted in little open space in Athens, as buildings erected in the last 40 years are too close to one another. There are also few trees to provide shade and beautify the streets.

Pollution has become a serious problem, especially with the increasing number of vehicles in the city. The combination of vehicle exhaust and industrial smoke produces an acidic smog that gets trapped inside the city by the mountains encircling Athens. This acidic smog, in the form of acid rain, eats away marble. Thus, one major concern about the smog is the harm it causes to the city's ancient monuments, most of which are made from marble.

Flea markets that cater to the tourist industry in Athens sell a large variety of souvenirs and handicrafts.

View from the White Tower, built in the 15th century, reveals a modern building complex facing the sea in the historical city of Thessaloníki, Greece's second largest.

THESSALONÍKI The second largest city in Greece, with a population of about 1.4 million, Thessaloníki is often called "the northern capital." It was founded in 315 B.C. by Kassandros, an army general who married Thessaloníki, Alexander the Great's stepsister.

Thessaloníki is surrounded by low hills facing an open bay. Because of its strategic location on the Aegean Sea, the city has been a prime target for invaders since ancient times. During the Turkish occupation of Greece, Thessaloníki outranked Athens in commercial and cultural importance. At the beginning of the 21st century, Thessaloníki was the second most important port and city in Greece.

Among Thessaloníki's many monuments are a triumphal arch erected in A.D. 303 by the Romans to honor Emperor Galerius. Via Egnatia was also built by the Romans to link Constantinople with Rome. After undergoing renovation in recent times, Via Egnatia continues to serve as the city's main road. Some Greek Christian art from the Byzantine era still survives in the city's churches.

PATRAS The third largest city in Greece and the main city of the Peloponnese, Patras has a population of 300,000. It is also the most important shipping center in western Greece, with ferry and container shipping links to the Ionian islands and Italy. Patras is also an important export center for currants, or dried Corinth raisins, which are shipped to Europe.

CLIMATE

The climate of Greece is Mediterranean. It is hot and dry in the summer but cool sea breezes make the heat bearable. Varying ranges of altitude and closeness to the sea, however, do result in differences in climate.

In the lowlands, summers are hot and dry, and winters are generally cold and damp. The average winter temperature in Athens is 50°F (10°C), but it can be colder in other parts of the country. In the northern region of Thessaloníki, the average temperature in January is 43°F (6°C). The colder northern climate is partly due to the bora, an icy wind that originates in the Balkan regions. Frost and snow are rare in the lowlands, but the mountains are covered with snow in the winter.

On the southern coast of Crete, it is warm enough to swim almost every day, and summer temperatures can reach 90°F (32°C). Still, snow remains on Crete's highest mountains all year round. The northern regions of Thrace, Macedonia, and Thessaly enjoy slightly cooler summers.

Rainfall also varies from region to region. Thessaly can have as little as 1.5 inches (3.8 cm) of rainfall per year, while parts of the western coast receive as much as 50 inches (127 cm) of rain per year.

As dusk falls on the island of Santorini, the bright daytime sunlight gives way to a soothing hue. Evenings are a time of leisure for most Greeks, who go out for long walks near the ocean to enjoy the cool sea breeze.

HISTORY

GREECE IS AN ANCIENT COUNTRY with a rich history of cultural and intellectual achievement. The remains of prehistoric humans dating back almost 100,000 years give evidence of the country's antiquity. Stories of ancient Greek civilizations are recounted in Greek literature.

EARLY CIVILIZATIONS

THE CYCLADIC CIVILIZATION Based in the Cyclades, this Bronze Age civilization flourished from 3000 to 1500 B.C. It was destroyed by a volcanic eruption on the island of Santorini around 1500 B.C.

THE MINOAN CIVILIZATION The Minoan civilization (3000–1400 B.C.) was centered on the island of Crete. Named after King Minos of Crete, this civilization was a peaceful sea power that traded with Syria, Spain, Egypt, and mainland Greece. The Minoans were sophisticated people who built beautiful cities and made use of technology unknown in neighboring cultures. The palace at Knossos, a Minoan city in Crete, had an indoor plumbing system.

The Minoan civilization came to an abrupt end around 1500 B.C., when the volcanic eruption in Santorini destroyed Knossos and other Minoan cities. The eruption did not completely wipe out Minoan culture, however. By this time, Minoan influence in architecture and the arts had spread to the Greek mainland.

Above: **This beautiful palace at Knossos in Crete dates to 2000 B.C.**

Opposite: **The Tholos, in Delphi, is one of the few circular buildings found in ancient Greek architecture. It was built in the 4th century B.C.**

Mycenae was the most important city during the Mycenaean period. The walls of this fortified city were made from huge slabs of stone. Years later, the Greeks believed the wall had been built by a mythological one-eyed giant called the Cyclops.

THE MYCENAEAN CIVILIZATION The Mycenaean civilization lasted from 1650 to 1150 B.C. and was based on the Peloponnesian peninsula.

The Myceneans were an advanced civilization. They built palaces and were skilled artisans. Many artifacts, such as crafted daggers, shields, death masks, and drinking cups, have been uncovered from Mycenaean ruins.

The Iliad, an epic story, tells of the Trojan War between the Greeks and the kingdom of Troy in Asia Minor. This war began when Paris, the prince of Troy, kidnapped Helen, the wife of the king of Sparta. Agamemnon, king of Mycenae, fought in this war, which eventually ended with the capture of Troy. It is believed this long war contributed to the collapse of the Mycenaean civilization around 1150 B.C.

The Greeks call this period of Mycenaean culture the Heroic Age of Greece, in honor of the Mycenaeans' courage.

THE DARK AGES The downfall of the Mycenaeans was brought about by the Dorians, a tribe from northern Greece. The Dorians used iron weapons that were superior to the bronze arms of the Mycenaeans.

The Dorian invasion was the beginning of an era of instability in Greece that lasted until about 800 B.C. Farming was in a state of disorder, trade was almost nonexistent, and there was a general decline in the arts. This period of Greek history is known as the Dark Ages.

THE CITY-STATES

The rise of the city-state, or *polis* ("POH-lees"), around 800 B.C. brought an end to the Dark Ages and marked the beginning of the Archaic Period.

City-states developed after isolated villages banded together under the authority of a particular city. Each city-state had its own system of government, industry, commerce, and culture. Corinth, Athens, Thebes, Delphi, Sparta, and Olympia were important city-states.

The Archaic Period was followed by the Classical Period, which lasted from 500 B.C. to 336 B.C. During this period Greek arts and sciences reached a high standard of achievement. The city-states were also the birthplace of the world's first democracies. The early city-states were ruled by kings. After 500 B.C., however, democratic governments developed, and free male citizens were allowed to serve in the government of the city-states.

During the Archaic period, the city-states faced the threat of invasion from the Persian empire in Asia Minor. In 490 B.C. King Darius of Persia fought the city-state of Athens on the plains of Marathon. Although the Persian army outnumbered the Athenians by almost four to one, the Athenians defeated the Persians, who lost over 6,000 men. The Greeks lost fewer than 200 men.

In 480 B.C. all the city-states united under the leadership of Athens and once again defeated the Persians in the battles of Salamis and Plataea. These Greek victories wiped out any future threat of Persian invasion.

Grave stele of a woman named Hegeso: the sculpture, created around 410 B.C., was originally part of a family burial plot. The sculpture shows a seated Hegeso looking at her jewelry box held in the hands of her slave girl.

Above: **The Parthenon on the Acropolis in Athens, built between 447 B.C. and 432 B.C., was the most beautiful temple in all of Greece. Every year, the ancient Greeks would hold a grand festival here to honor Athena, the goddess of wisdom and the mythical founder of the city of Athens.**

Opposite: **Six graceful statues serve as columns in the Eréchtheum on the Acropolis. Built in 395 B.C., the temple was used as a church by the Crusaders in the Middle Ages. The Ottoman Turks later used the temple as a mansion during the Ottoman occupation of Greece.**

THE GOLDEN AGE OF ATHENS

Athens emerged as the political and cultural center of Greece following the defeat of the Persians. In the peaceful years that followed, democracy and the arts flourished. Athenian accomplishments in science, the arts, philosophy, and architecture during this period, called the Golden Age of Athens, set the standard for later European civilizations.

The Golden Age of Greek literature was marked by Hesiod's poems and Homer's epic poems *The Iliad* and *The Odyssey*. Greek theater reached great heights with the tragic Athenian plays of Aeschylus, Sophocles, and Euripides, and the comedies of Aristophanes.

In architecture, many beautiful structures, like the Parthenon of Athens, were built. This was also the age of great thinkers. Socrates and Plato devoted their lives to the pursuit of truth and knowledge. Aristotle, Plato's student, made enormous contributions to science and philosophy.

Athenian supremacy was later challenged by Sparta, a rival city-state. In 431 B.C., the Peloponnesian Wars broke out between the city-states. The wars lasted 27 years. Athens was defeated, and Sparta ruled Greece for a short time. Sparta was later defeated by the city-state of Thebes, which was quickly overthrown. The wars greatly weakened the Greek city-states.

PERICLES

Pericles was a famous statesman who helped shape Athenian democracy. Born to a noble family around 490 B.C., Pericles strongly believed in democracy and the rights of the ordinary citizen. He believed that all citizens should be involved in the process of government and put his ideas into practice.

Pericles established the Delian League—an alliance of city-states dedicated to the protection of one another. In 454 B.C., Athens seized the treasury of the Delian League, and eventually all members of the League were forced to become part of the Athenian empire. Athens grew to be the center of Greek civilization and produced many great cultural achievements. Under the initiative of Pericles, the Parthenon and other temples were built.

Pericles and his contributions were so vital to the growth and prosperity of Athens that this time has also been called the Age of Pericles.

Alexander the Great was not only a brilliant military leader, he was instructed in philosophy, medicine, and science by the great Greek philosopher Aristotle.

MACEDONIA

In the middle of the fourth century B.C., King Phillip II of Macedonia in northern Greece attacked and captured the weakened Greek city-states. Phillip greatly admired the cultural developments of the city-states; his goal was to build a huge Greek army and spread Greek civilization to other lands, such as Persia. Phillip was assassinated in 336 B.C. before he could realize this dream.

Phillip's son, Alexander, carried on his father's plans and became one of the greatest soldiers and conquerors of all time. Although he came to the throne at the age of 20 and ruled for only 13 years, Alexander the Great, as he became known, created one of the largest empires in the ancient world. He conquered the vast Persian empire, Egypt, and lands as far east as northern India.

The success of Alexander's campaigns was mostly due to his cavalry, a group of about 5,000 armed horsemen. A military formation called the phalanx—a solid, moving wall of foot soldiers bearing shields and long spears— also played an important role in his victories. Alexander's father, Phillip, had also used the phalanx to defeat the city-states.

After Alexander died in 323 B.C. at the age of 33, his great empire collapsed. Parts of his empire became independent city-states. Other parts became independent kingdoms, such as Syria, Egypt, and Macedonia. Alexander's legacy, however, lived on in the city of Alexandria in Egypt, which became a center of learning. By the time of Alexander's death, Greek culture had spread to almost all the lands that he had conquered. After Alexander's death, Macedonia controlled Greece for 200 years.

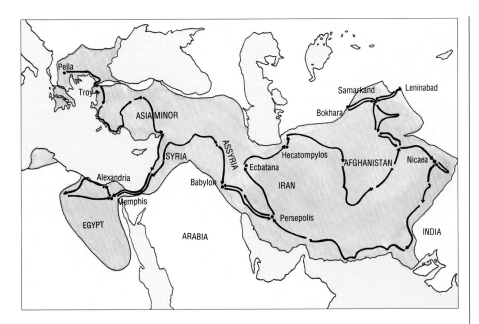

The Macedonian empire of Alexander the Great. The arrows trace the route of Alexander in his 13-year campaign, in which he created a vast empire covering over 1 million square miles (2.6 million square km).

ROMAN AND BYZANTINE EMPIRES

In 146 B.C., the powerful Roman Empire conquered Greece. The Greeks welcomed the Romans, whom they regarded as the "protectors of Greek freedom." The Romans treated the Greeks with respect out of their great admiration for Greek intellectual and cultural life. Greece prospered once again, and Greek art and culture continued to thrive during this period.

Roman culture was greatly influenced by Greek culture. In mythology, the Roman gods were based on the Greek gods. When Christianity spread, the Greeks were among the first converts, and the Gospels were first written in Greek.

In A.D. 285, Emperor Diocletian decided to share the throne of the vast Roman empire. He ruled the eastern half of the empire and appointed another emperor to rule the western half. Although in theory the empire was still one, in practice, it had become divided. The western half was Latin-speaking, while the eastern half was Greek-speaking.

Constantine succeeded Diocletian in A.D. 312. In A.D. 324, Constantine moved the capital of the empire from Rome to the city of Byzantium. The western empire fell to Germanic tribes in A.D. 476. The eastern empire flourished independently and came to be known as the Byzantine empire.

Byzantine art is famous for the paintings of saints, called icons, found inside the churches.

THE BYZANTINE EMPIRE After the death of Emperor Constantine, Byzantium was renamed Constantinople in his honor. For nearly nine centuries, from A.D. 330 to 1204, Constantinople remained the capital of the Byzantine empire. The empire was Greek in culture and language, but its laws and administration were based on Roman practices.

In 394 Emperor Theodosius I declared Christianity the official religion in Greece and forbade the worship of Greek and Roman gods, which he regarded as paganism.

Justinian the Great (A.D. 527–565) was the most famous Byzantine emperor. He wanted to restore the former glory of the ancient Roman empire to the Byzantine empire. Although the empire under his control was far smaller than ancient Rome, he was able to expand his control to northern Africa, Italy, and parts of Spain. Under Justinian's rule, Christian theology replaced the study of classical Greek philosophy as the highest form of scholarship. Beautiful churches, such as the Hagia Sophia, or Great Church, in Constantinople, were built during this time.

An old Venetian fort in Greece. This is one of many monuments built during the Crusades, a series of wars waged by Christian European rulers and the Pope to liberate the Holy Land from Muslim conquerors. The Crusades took place between the 11th and the 13th centuries.

Emperor Justinian is also famous for codifying the Roman Law, *Codex Justinianus*, which bears his name.

FRANKISH AND VENETIAN OCCUPATION

In 1204, the Fourth Crusade from Europe tore the Byzantine empire apart. Constantinople was plundered, and the Aegean islands and Greek mainland fell to the Frankish crusaders and their Venetian allies.

Although Constantinople was freed 55 years later, much of Greece and the Aegean islands remained under Frankish and Venetian occupation. Greece was divided into small states controlled by various Frankish and Venetian administrators.

By the mid-1400s the Ottoman Turks from Anatolia (now in Turkey) had advanced on Greece, conquering each of the city-states. In 1453 Constantinople was captured by the Turks, marking the end of the Byzantine empire and the beginning of Turkish domination of Greece.

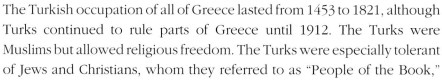

TURKISH RULE

During the 400 years of Ottoman Turkish rule, Christianity continued to be practiced in Greece in Byzantine monasteries.

The Turkish occupation of all of Greece lasted from 1453 to 1821, although Turks continued to rule parts of Greece until 1912. The Turks were Muslims but allowed religious freedom. The Turks were especially tolerant of Jews and Christians, whom they referred to as "People of the Book," people who worshiped one God and had a written scripture. The Turks were more tolerant of other religions than the Roman Catholic Franks and Venetians had been. Turkish rule, however, was oppressive. The Turks imposed heavy taxes, forced one out of every five male Greek children to enlist in the Turkish army after converting him to Islam, killed groups of Greek men that they thought might lead a revolution, and engaged in numerous wars with Venice, using Greece as a battleground.

The Greeks suffered poverty under Turkish rule. Turkish oppression, however, led to the strengthening of Greek ethnic pride. Greek culture, language, and beliefs were preserved by the Eastern Orthodox Church, and the Church came to represent Greek nationalism.

INDEPENDENCE

By the 1820s, the Turkish Ottoman empire was losing control of its vast territory. In 1821 the Greeks began a revolt that eventually led to the Greek War of Independence.

In 1827 French, Russian, and British forces joined Greece in its fight against the Turks. In 1829 the Turkish sultan signed a treaty recognizing Greek independence.

MONARCHY

In 1830 the Great, or Protective, Powers of Britain, France, and Russia signed the Treaty of London. The treaty established a Greek kingdom made up of the mainland south of Thessaly, the Peloponnese, the Aegean islands, and the island of Euboea. In order to avoid a power struggle among the Greeks, the Great Powers decided to place a foreign king on the throne of Greece.

In 1833 Prince Otto of Bavaria was crowned king of Greece. Although popular at the start of his reign, Otto lost the support of the Greek people and was deposed in 1862. The Great Powers replaced him with Prince William of Denmark, who was crowned King George I, and a new liberal and democratic constitution was enacted.

King George II (1890–1947) ruled Greece during the turbulent years between the two world wars.

King George I regained Greece's traditional territory with the acquisition of the Ionian islands from the British, and Thessaly and southern Epirus from the Ottoman Turks. In 1912, after emerging victorious in the Balkan Wars, Greece reclaimed Epirus, Macedonia, Crete, and several islands.

King George I was assassinated in 1913. His successor, King Constantine, disagreed with his charismatic prime minister, Eleutherios Venizélos, over Greece's role in World War I. The rivalry between king and prime minister divided the Greek population into two—one side supporting Constantine, and the other, Venizélos. Constantine was ousted and, under Venizélos's authority, Greece joined the war in 1917 on the side of the Great Powers.

George Papadopoulos (1919–99) was the junta leader that overthrew the Greek government in 1967. He served as prime minister of Greece from 1967 to 1973.

DICTATORSHIP AND WAR

King Constantine returned to power in 1920 with much public support. The victory of the Allies and the defeat of the Ottoman Turks in World War I granted Greece the opportunity to reclaim territory from Turkey. However, the Greeks were bitterly defeated by the Turks in Anatolia in 1922. The king was blamed for this defeat and forced into exile. His son and successor, King George II, reigned until 1924, when Greece became a republic for a short period. In 1935 King George II was called back, as many Greeks still supported the monarchy.

With the king's consent, a military dictator, Ioánnis Metaxas, suspended the constitution in August 1936 and ruled Greece until 1940. When Italy invaded Greece during World War II, Greek forces, under Alexandros Papagos, drove back the much larger Italian army. The Greek army, however, was unable to hold off the German invasion in 1941, and Greece was occupied by Nazi forces.

When the Germans withdrew from Greece in 1944, the country's economy was in ruins and famine was widespread. Communist forces tried to take control of Greece but were defeated in a civil war that ended in 1949. The monarchy returned to power, and the Greek economy received aid from the United States. In 1952 Prime Minister Alexandros Papagos began the reconstruction of the country.

In the 1950s, Cyprus, a British colony where the majority of the population was Greek, became the object of a dispute between Greece and Turkey. Britain granted Cyprus independence in 1960, after tense negotiations with Greece, Turkey, and Cyprus.

From 1952 to 1963, an authoritative regime ruled Greece. After a short period of rule by the Center Union Party, a group of military colonels led by Colonel George Papadopoulos overthrew the government in 1967. Civil rights were suspended and the monarchy was abolished. A new constitution was drawn up providing for a stable government but eliminating political freedom.

DEMOCRACY

In June 1973 Papadopoulos proclaimed Greece a republic and announced plans for parliamentary elections. In November of the same year, another group of military officers overthrew the Papadopoulos government.

In 1974 the Greek military tried to overthrow the government of Cyprus. Turkey sent troops to the island, but both countries signed a ceasefire a few days later.

The military government collapsed after the failed takeover of Cyprus and growing economic problems. Constantine Karamanlis, a former prime minister, was called to head the new government in 1974. Parliamentary elections were held in November of that year, followed by a referendum to make the country a republic.

From 1981 to 1989 the Panhellenic Socialist Movement (PASOK) controlled parliament with Andreas Papandreou as prime minister. In 1990 the New Democratic Party came to power but was defeated by PASOK in the 1992 election. Papandreou became prime minister once again but retired in 1996. Constantine Simitis succeeded Papandreou and was reelected in April 2001.

Andreas Papandreou (1919–96) was the son of George Papandreou, former prime minister of Greece. He founded PASOK, the socialist party that continues to rule Greece.

GOVERNMENT

GREECE HAS BEEN A PARLIAMENTARY republic since 1974. In that year, a new constitution was put into effect, providing for civil liberties and individual rights, which had been abolished during the years of military and authoritative regime. The constitution was amended in 2001.

ADMINISTRATIVE STRUCTURE

According to the Greek constitution, the president is the head of state and the supreme commander of the armed forces. Unlike in the United States, the president is not elected by the people; the Greek parliament appoints the president for a five-year term. Since the president is elected by the political majority in parliament, the president is unlikely to challenge any decisions made by the parliament members. The powers of the president are mainly ceremonial. However, with the consent of the Greek parliament, the president may declare war and sign international agreements concerning peace, alliance, and participation in international organizations. The president may serve a maximum of two terms.

The Greek parliament, or *Vouli* ("VOO-lee"), consists of 300 members, or deputies, who hold office for four years. Members of parliament are elected by the people. The head of the majority political party in parliament is appointed prime minister. Political power lies in the hands of the prime minister. The current prime minister is Constantine Simitis and the current president is Constantine Stephanopoulos.

The Greek Supreme Court handles criminal and civil cases. The Supreme Special Tribunal is the highest court of law in Greece; it deals with constitutional issues and ensures that parliamentary elections are valid. The president, in consultation with a judicial council, appoints its members.

Greek citizens 18 years old and above are required by law to vote in all elections. Voting is done through the secret ballot.

The birthplace of democracy, Greece has also experienced undemocratic governments in the course of its history. It is sometimes said that Greek civilization has been around for so long that it has had a chance to try nearly every form of government.

Opposite: **Two Greek evzones ("EV-zones"), or soldiers, in traditional uniform march in front of the presidential palace.**

PARLIAMENT AND THE MONARCHY

In the 19th century, during the fight for independence from Turkish rule, many Greeks joined different political parties. Each party embraced a different political ideology, so the formation of a new and independent government would not have united these factions. The Great Powers of Britain, France, and Russia, decided then that the best way to avoid political turmoil in Greece was to make the country a monarchy and make a foreigner king. Thus the Greek monarchy was born.

Although the Greeks did not object to their foreign king in the beginning, they later questioned the role of the monarchy. In 1844 attempts to curb the absolute power of the king led to the adoption of a constitution that established a legislature. By 1862 discontent led to a second revolt and King Otto was deposed. The new liberal and democratic constitution of 1864 established a new monarchy under King George I. The constitution called for the creation of a unicameral (one-house) legislature based on representation by vote and very limited powers for the king.

Between the 1860s and 1952, parliament reverted to a two-house body and then back again to a one-house body.

George Papadopoulos addressing the Greek parliament in 1967. The "parliament" during the rule of the junta was not elected by the people; its members were chosen by leading members of the government.

The issue of whether Greece should continue to have a monarchy was finally resolved in the constitution of 1975, when the monarchy was abolished. King Constantine II was Greece's last king.

DICTATORSHIP AND DEMOCRACY

After the defeat of the communists in 1949, a right-wing government ruled Greece from 1952 to 1963. The government retained its power by repressing political freedom and persecuting its opponents. The population grew discontented with the authoritative regime and sought reform.

In 1964 the Center Union Party, headed by George Papandreou, won the parliamentary elections and came to power. Although Papandreou tried to bring social reform to Greece, his rule did not succeed in putting a stop to the years of riots, strikes, and political fighting. The military stepped in to take full control in April 1967.

The military dictatorship lasted until 1974, when the Greek military's attempt to overthrow the government of Cyprus met with defeat. The ruling military junta lost the support of senior military officers, who called for Karamanlis, a former prime minister, to return from exile. A new constitution came into effect in June 1975 and established a republic.

Greek soldiers take part in an annual parade to commemorate the joint holidays of the Annunciation of the Virgin Mary and Independence Day on March 25.

ARMED FORCES

Greece is protected by an army, an air force, and a navy. Greek men must serve from one year to 18 months in any branch of the armed forces. The government spends 6 percent of the annual gross domestic product (GDP) on the military.

Until the late 1990s, the greatest threat to Greek security was Turkey, as the two nations have had historical disputes over Cyprus and other territory for decades. The devastating earthquakes that hit both countries in 1999 helped improve relations, when each country came to the aid of the other.

POLITICAL PARTIES

Greece's two main political parties are the Panhellenic Socialist Movement (PASOK) and the New Democracy party, both founded in 1974. Other parties are the Communist Party of Greece and the United Left Alliance.

The PASOK government ruled Greece for most of the 1980s and 1990s, except for a brief period of coalition governments and New Democracy rule in the late 1980s and early 1990s. The PASOK government brought about significant social reform in Greece—women acquired equal rights, the voting age was lowered to 18, and civil marriage was legalized.

Political parties in Greece are closely associated with the personality of a strong leader. Andreas Papandreou was PASOK's driving force. He remained a key figure in Greek politics until his death in 1996. In the 2000 election, PASOK won by a narrow margin. Constantine Simitis became prime minister and Constantine Stephanopoulos president.

CYPRUS

The island of Cyprus is the third largest island in the Mediterranean. Cyprus has an area of 3,572 square miles (9,251 square km) and a population of about 800,000.

The Greeks and the Turks are the two main ethnic groups in Cyprus. The Greek-speaking people have lived on the island since the days prior to Alexander the Great. Turkish Cypriots are the descendants of the Ottoman Turks who conquered the island in 1571 and occupied it until 1878, when Britain assumed control of Cyprus. In 1960 Cyprus gained its independence. In 1974 hostilities broke out between the two ethnic groups and the island was divided—today, two-thirds of Cyprus is occupied by Greek troops, and the northern one-third is occupied by Turkish forces.

The constitution of Cyprus stipulates that the vice-president of the republic and 24 of the 80 members of the House of Representatives must be Turkish. The two communities are self-governing with regard to education, culture, and religion. All matters pertaining to government fall under the jurisdiction of the joint administration.

However, since February 1975, the post of vice-president and 24 seats in the House of Representatives have been vacant, as Turkish Cypriots formed their own government in 1975. The Turkish Cypriot government is not recognized by the United Nations.

ECONOMY

GREECE'S MAIN ECONOMIC activities are shipping, tourism, manufacturing, and agriculture. Considered to be one of the EU's poorest countries, Greece has posted economic growth in the last few years. Foreign capital invested in the country has encouraged the development of new industries and the creation of jobs. Further growth is expected to come from the service sector and the tourist industry. Agriculture, on the other hand, is expected to decline in importance.

Greece's potential for economic growth has been thwarted by years of war, civil unrest, and authoritative regimes. At the end of World War II, many Greek industries lay in ruins. With help from the United States, Greece's economy improved in the 1950s. From the mid-1960s to the mid-1970s, Greece's economy grew by an annual average of 10 percent. Personal spending increased and the standard of living improved.

In 1981 Greece became the 10th member of the European Community (EC, later renamed EU, or European Union), a group of Western European nations that sought to unite their resources to make one strong economy. Greece's membership in the EU has been a positive boost for the economy. The agricultural sector has benefitted from subsidies, Greece has received aid to carry out infrastructure projects, and the industrial sector has grown.

The Greek economy grew by 3.8 percent in 2000. Its average agricultural and industrial output still lags behind that of other EU nations, and despite talk of privatization, the Greek government continues to exercise control over key industries such as banking, aerospace, and telecommunications.

Above: **The dry climate of Greece is ideal for cultivating cotton.**

Opposite: **A sponge seller carries his merchandise in the streets of Athens. Greece is a leading producer of sea sponges.**

TOURISM

Tourism is the fastest-growing industry in Greece; it accounts for a large portion of the country's annual GDP and shows potential for further growth. About 12 million tourists visit Greece each year, more than the country's entire population.

Beautiful beaches, plentiful sunshine, and breathtaking islands, in addition to the country's matchless cultural heritage, have made Greece a favorite vacation spot. Most of the tourists come from Europe. In the summer, during peak season, from mid-June to the end of August, the tourist industry employs about 8 percent of the entire labor force. This figure decreases sharply during the off-season, from the end of November to the beginning of April, when most of the tourist facilities are unused.

Over the past 50 years, the Greek government has tried to improve the condition of the roads in Greece, making travel easier. Still, the standard of general infrastructure remains far behind that of most other EU countries.

AGRICULTURE

Agriculture employs 20 percent of the labor force in Greece, but it accounts for only 8 percent of the GDP. Poor soil, low rainfall, and an inefficient system of small landownership have played a part in keeping agriculture from becoming a profitable industry.

Because of the shortage of arable land (only 30 percent of the total land area), Greece does not produce enough grain to feed its population and must import food from other countries. Nevertheless, Greece is a major exporter of cotton and tobacco to the EU. Wheat, oats, millet, and barley are native to Greece.

Olives, grown mainly for olive oil, and grapes, from which juice and wine are made, are also important crops. Currants are another grape product. In fact, the word "currant" is derived from the phrase "Corinth grape." Other fruits include apricots, dates, figs, oranges, and peaches.

Livestock is raised in pastures and meadows. However, due to the lack of rich pasture, Greek livestock is of poor quality. Greece imports most of its meat.

Since joining the EU, Greece has received subsidies aimed at improving the agricultural sector. However, as the rural population moves to the cities to find jobs, the economic role of agriculture may continue to decline.

OLIVES

Greece is the world's third leading producer of olives, which flourish in the country's dry climate. The ancient Greeks believed that the goddess Athena had presented Athens with an olive plant and that its cultivation would make the people prosperous. Olive plantations cover the whole of the Peloponnese and much of Sterea Ellas, Crete, and Thessaly.

Hundreds of different types of olive trees are grown in Greece. Some varieties are grown for food, others for producing olive oil. The majority of the olive trees in Greece produce olives for olive oil.

In the spring, farmers prune the olive trees and use the trimmings for fuel. Several weeks later small white flowers appear that transform into the familiar hard green fruit. Later in the season, families go out with long poles to knock down the green olives. Green olives are usually exported. Greeks prefer the ripe black olives available later in the season.

The black olive harvest officially begins in November. Sheets are spread beneath the trees, and pickers on ladders run their hands over the loaded branches. The ripe fruit falls to the sheets; the unripe olives remain on the branches to mature. Several weeks later, the procedure is repeated, and continues throughout winter. The harvest is usually completed in February.

Olives to be eaten are usually pickled in barrels of brine. Olives that are grown for their oil are crushed immediately after picking.

FISHING

The Greeks have practiced fishing and sponge-diving since ancient times. In present-day Greece, more than 50,000 people continue to make a living as fishermen. They work either on fishing boats or at canneries and food processing centers near the ports.

The Aegean Sea is rich in fish. Nearly 250 species of fish are found in Greek waters, including bass, carp, cod, mackerel, perch, red mullet, swordfish, lobster, and shrimp. In recent years, overfishing and inefficient fish stock conservation have damaged the fishing industry, so Greece must import many fish products.

Sponge-fishing has a long tradition in Greece, particularly on the Dodecanese islands. As uncontrolled harvesting has depleted the traditional fishing areas, divers sometimes go as far as the North African coast to fish for sponges. While at sea, fishermen tear off the sponges' outer membrane to prevent decay. Final trimming, drying, and grading is done at the port.

A Greek fisherman and his wife clean their nets after a day at sea. The harvest from the seas around Greece used to be rich and plentiful because the warm waters encouraged the growth of plankton, the basic food supply for fish. Lately, the harvest has diminished greatly due to overfishing.

Greek ships travel all over the world, from Europe and Africa to Asia and the Americas.

A LEADER IN SHIPPING

Shipping is a vital part of the Greek economy, providing more than 100,000 jobs. With over 5,000 ships, Greece's merchant fleet is one of the largest in the world although Greek ships are generally older than the world average. Greek ships make up 70 percent of the European Union's total merchant fleet.

Greece also has a large shipbuilding and ship refitting industry. Its six shipyards near Piraeus are among the biggest in Europe.

As Greek ships primarily transport cargo between third-world countries, international economic trends have a serious impact on the Greek shipping industry. Pleasure cruise liners, a part of both the tourist industry and the shipping industry, are also affected by economic downturns and world events.

Finding enough people to work on the ships is also an issue in the industry. According to Greek law, 75 percent of a ship's crew must be Greek. However, the lonely life at sea attracts few workers, so ship owners are obliged to provide excellent benefits and pay higher salaries than they may be able to afford in order to attract people to work on the ships.

INDUSTRY

Industrialization was given a boost when Greece joined the European Community in 1981. As foreign capital flowed into the country, new factories were set up. Government policies have supported the growth of new industries such as food processing and the production of telecommunications equipment. Industrial activity has risen steadily for the past 10 years, accounting for 21 percent of the country's GDP.

Athens and Thessaloníki are the main industrial centers. Greece's main manufactured products are cement, steel, chemicals, electrical equipment, cigarettes, textiles, clothing, and processed foods.

Historically, Greek manufacturing developed out of small artisan businesses. There are still many businesses and cottage industries that have fewer than 10 employees and depend on labor more than equipment to produce goods such as textiles, clothing, and footwear.

A traditional Greek stonemason at work.

MINING

Minerals are one of the few natural resources available in Greece in considerable quantity. In the 1980s, more than 22,000 workers were employed in mining. However, with the exception of lignite, a brownish-black coal, and bauxite, an ore that is the principal source of aluminum, most Greek mines operate below their production capacity.

About 90 percent of mined lignite is used to generate electricity. Lignite is found mainly on the island of Euboea, in the central Peloponnese, and in the Ptolemais basin in the Pindus mountains.

Other minerals found in Greece include chromite, zinc, lead, copper, asbestos, and magnesite. The Aegean Sea may be a source of offshore petroleum but Greece and Turkey continue to dispute ownership.

THE EUROPEAN UNION

The European Union (EU) was formed with the signing of the Treaty on European Union in Maastricht, the Netherlands, in February 1992. The Maastricht Treaty was signed by representatives from Belgium, Denmark, France, Germany, Greece, Ireland, Italy, Luxembourg, the Netherlands, Portugal, Spain, and the United Kingdom.

The treaty was the latest step on the road to European integration that began in the 1950s with the formation of the European Economic Community (EEC), also known as the Common Market. Later, the EEC was referred to as the European Community (EC).

The EU hopes to boost the economic situation of its member countries by creating a general tariff on imports, thus protecting EU industries from foreign competition. Companies are also allowed to invest in any member country without trade restrictions.

The EU also encourages mobility and social integration among its citizens, as they are allowed to reside and settle in any of the member countries. Issues such as consumer protection, public health, education, industrial policy, foreign policy, security, and environmental protection are handled by a common EU governing body.

GREECE AND THE EU

Greece joined the EC in 1981 and was one of the signatories of the Maastricht Treaty. The government of Greece, one of the least developed economies in the union, implemented reform programs in order to shape up the economy for membership in the Economic and Monetary Union (EMU). The programs were successful, and Greece became a member on January 1, 2001. The euro became Greece's official currency on January 1, 2002 (*above: Prime Minister Simitis, second from right, holds a newly minted sheet of Greek euros*).

Greece has benefited from EU financial aid in the following ways:
- In 2001, 3.4 percent of Greece's GDP consisted of EU financial aid.
- Agriculture, though small in scale, has received a boost. The EU is subsidizing Greek agricultural products in order to make them more competitive in the European market.
- Between 1994 and 2006, Greece will have received US$24 billion in structural funds aimed at modernizing the transportation system in time for the 2004 Olympic Games, which will be held in Athens. A more extensive subway system and the new international airport, both in Athens, opened in 2001.

ENVIRONMENT

GREECE IS A MOUNTAINOUS COUNTRY nearly surrounded by the sea. In spite of its size, about the same as Alabama, Greece boasts a variety of ecosystems, each supporting unique flora and fauna. Rugged mountain ranges averaging over 5,000 feet (1,500 m) in height cover about 70 percent of the total land area of the country, including the islands, making most of Greece's terrain uneven.

Greece's climate, in turn, is a reflection of the ruggedness of its terrain and, though largely Mediterranean, it ranges from semi-arid in the southern islands to cold and wet in the northern mountains near the border with Bulgaria.

Differences in terrain and climate have made it possible for many of Greece's plant and animal species to develop in relative isolation. Greece has 6,000 recorded species of plants, some of which are endemic, or present only in Greece, including more than 100 varieties of orchid. Forests of birch, pine, and spruce grow in the cold northern region. Many of these forests have been damaged by uncontrolled goat grazing, felling, and forest fires.

Greece's varied wildlife, one of the richest in Europe, includes 116 mammal species, 18 species of amphibians, 59 species of reptiles, 240 bird species, and 107 species of fish. It is estimated that about half of the endemic mammal species are in danger of becoming extinct. Unique species of sea turtles and monk seals, now found in large colonies only in Greek waters, have decreased dramatically over the past few decades.

Greece is home to the Ambracian Gulf Wetlands Reserve, located in the southwestern area of Epirus. Its rare ecosystem, protected by the international RAMSAR treaty, houses the last examples of riverbank woodlands as well as one of the last colonies of silver pelicans in Europe.

Above: **Greece is home to a great variety of endemic fauna, such as the tree frog in Crete.**

Opposite: **The soil of Greece's rich forests has been eroded by uncontrolled cultivation of profitable crops, such as olive trees.**

47

ENDANGERED SPECIES

Nearly completely surrounded by the sea, Greece is endowed with a rich and varied marine population, from abundant fish to seals, dolphins, and turtles. Over the last few decades, Greece's marine life has declined sharply due to overfishing, uncontrolled tourist activities, water pollution, and deliberate killings by fishermen, who regard seals and dolphins as competitors in the hunt for fish.

The *Monachus monachus*, or monk seal, is a part of Greece's natural and cultural heritage. The monk seal is described basking on Greece's sandy shores by Homer in his epic poem *The Odyssey*. The head of a monk seal was even found carved on a coin dated 500 B.C. Once found in large colonies, only 250 monk seals are estimated left in Greek waters. Dolphins and turtles in the Mediterranean Sea also face extinction.

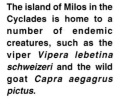

The island of Milos in the Cyclades is home to a number of endemic creatures, such as the viper *Vipera lebetina schweizeri* and the wild goat *Capra aegagrus pictus*.

Not only are some of Greece's marine creatures in danger of extinction, its land animals are also increasingly threatened by the damaging effects of pollution and interbreeding. The wild goat of Antimilos, an islet in the southwestern Cyclades, is a rare species unique to Antimilos. This goat has brown fur and a black stripe on its back; it is threatened by hybridization, or interbreeding, with domesticated goats.

The island of Milos and surrounding islets in the Cyclades have a number of endemic reptiles and amphibians. Milos supports 90 percent of the total population of a unique viper species. A rare lizard also lives on Milos and other nearby islands. During the reproductive period the male becomes strongly colored with blue spots on its sides. Milos also serves as a passageway for birds migrating from Africa to Europe.

The Greek government and the EU have passed legislation to protect the endemic creatures of the Cyclades from the threat of extinction.

A rescue team saves the last surviving sea turtle in a group of four that were found tangled in a discarded fishing net in Greek waters.

THE MONK SEAL

The Mediterranean monk seal, or *Monachus monachus* (*below*), is Europe's number-one endangered marine mammal and one of the six most endangered mammals in the world. Once present throughout the Mediterranean, the Marmara, and Black seas, and along the Atlantic coast of Africa, monk seals have been reduced to around 400, of which about 250 live in Greek waters.

The ancient Greeks hunted monk seals to obtain products that were essential to their survival, such as fur, oil, meat, and medicines. However, the numbers they hunted were never large enough to threaten the species with extinction. During the time of the Roman empire and later in the Middle Ages, the population of monk seals was almost depleted due to excessive commercial hunting. The remaining monk seal population retreated from the beaches and rocks to inaccessible caves with underwater entrances. Present-day female monk seals choose caves or other undisturbed places to give birth to pups.

Human activity is the main threat to the survival of the monk seal today. Monk seals die when they get caught in fishing nets. Fishermen sometimes deliberately kill the monk seals, which they consider a competitor in the hunt for fish. Pollution caused by ships (oil leaks, run-off, and sewage) and uncontrolled tourism (which leads to the encroachment of human settlement into animal habitats) are destroying the monk seal's natural environment.

The island complex of Milos-Antimilos-Kimolos-Polyaigos has been set apart by the EU as a reserve, as monk seal shelters have been identified along the shores and newborn pups have been spotted in the area during the reproductive period. This initiative is part of Natura 2000, an EU program to create a network of protected areas to preserve endangered species and their habitats.

AIR POLLUTION

According to Greece's Ministry of Public Works and Environment (PEHODE), the country produces 5.2 million tons of solid waste and 1,500 tons of hazardous waste per year.

Most of the garbage is collected and disposed of in the country's 5,000 landfill sites. As there is no treatment or separation of waste prior to incineration, burning garbage at these landfills releases dioxin, a harmful chemical pollutant, into the atmosphere. There are only two sanitary landfills in Greece, on the islands of Zákinthos and Lemnos, where biogas and harmful chemicals are treated before they are released into the atmosphere.

Air pollution is a major environmental problem. The air in Athens, in particular, is degraded by exhaust from automobiles. In the summer, vehicular traffic is responsible for about 80 percent of the smog in Athens. Diesel-run vehicles, such as taxis, buses, and trucks, are major contributors to air pollution. With a new subway system in Athens and the modernization of the country's transportation system with aid from the EU, people's reliance on highly-polluting vehicles for transportation should gradually decrease.

Growing industrial cities such as Thessaloníki and Piraeus are also facing the problem of air pollution due to poor waste disposal methods.

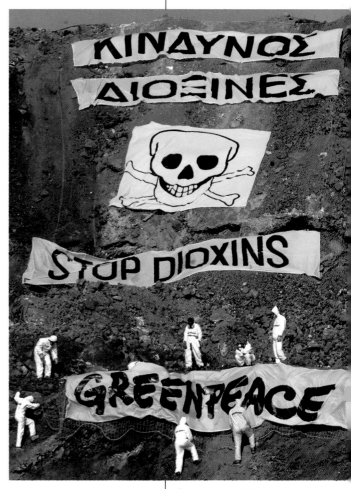

Greenpeace activists at a waste dump area protest the disposal of industrial waste with high levels of dioxin from a steel recycling plant in Athens.

THE LOGGERHEAD SEA TURTLE

Greece is home to the last remaining nesting sites in the Mediterranean for the rare loggerhead sea turtle (*below*). Every year, Laganas Bay on Zákinthos, an island in the Ionian Sea, off the northwestern shore of the Peloponnese, hosts 1,300 nests along 8 miles (5 km) of beach. Loggerhead sea turtles are large but gentle creatures that can weigh up to 350 pounds (159 kg).

Although they spend most of their life in the sea, loggerhead sea turtles return to their nesting beaches to lay their eggs. From the end of May until the end of August, loggerheads from different parts of the Mediterranean return to the beaches of Zákinthos. The female comes ashore at night to lay about 120 ping-pong ball-like eggs in the sand, and after covering the 20- to 24-inch- (50- to 60-cm-) deep nest, she returns to the sea. The female loggerhead may return 15 days later to dig another nest and may repeat this process three or four times in one season.

The eggs must remain undisturbed in the warm sand for about 60 days before they hatch. After the eggs hatch, the hatchlings remain in the nest for several days. From late July until the end of October, the hatchlings start to emerge from their nests. They dig their way out of the nest in a joint effort, usually streaming out at night. The hatchlings then make their way down to the sea. The race from their nest to the sea is crucial to their survival, as predators may be waiting nearby. Although a female sea turtle may lay hundreds of eggs each summer, it is estimated that only a small number of hatchlings will survive to adulthood.

Most female loggerheads return to their nesting beaches after 2 or 3 years to repeat the nesting cycle. It is thus crucial to the survival of the loggerhead sea turtle that these nests be protected from pollutants or other disturbances such as human intrusion. Zákinthos has been selected to become a protected reserve under the Natura 2000 program run by the EU.

Young Greeks take part in the Europe Car Free Day in Athens on September 22, 2001. The event aims to reduce exhaust from vehicular traffic in Athens.

CONSERVATION EFFORTS

Greek nongovernmental organizations (NGOs) and environmental groups supported by the EU are alerting Greek and other European citizens to the plight of the environment in Greece.

MO'M The Hellenic Society for the Study and Protection of the Monk Seal was established in 1988 by a group of marine biologists and researchers. The aim of this NGO is to gain knowledge about the monk seal species by study and research, and to protect the monk seal by all legal means possible. MO'M is funded by membership dues and contributions from more than 5,500 supporters. MO'M also enjoys the support of the EU and has been a member of the International Union for the Conservation of Nature (IUCN) since 1996.

ARCHELON The Sea Turtle Protection Society of Greece is a nonprofit organization founded in 1983. Archelon monitors an average of 2,500 nests a year in the major nesting areas, such as Zákinthos, and runs public awareness and environmental education programs. In 1994 Archelon set up the first Sea Turtle Rescue Center in the Mediterranean, which receives and treats sick and injured turtles from all over Greece.

GREEKS

THE POPULATION OF GREECE is nearly homogeneous. According to government statistics, about 98 percent of the people are ethnic Greeks. The remaining 2 percent are Turks, Vlachs, Slavs, Albanians, Jews, and Gypsies.

Over the last decade, thousands of immigrants have come to Greece from former communist bloc countries, such as Albania, in search of work, but their numbers have not been included in official population statistics.

GREEK PERSONALITY

The Greeks, or Hellenes, have a complex personality, which may be the result of the many years of Roman, Frankish, and Turkish domination of Greece.

Traditionally, their Hellenic background is believed to account for the Greeks' lack of materialism, search for ideals, respect for the law, reliance on logic for making decisions and for advancement, and preference for Western European dance and music.

But the Greek personality also has a practical side that focuses on reality, makes decisions on matters concerning money and power, bypasses rules to achieve goals, values education, and loves the country lifestyle and its folk music.

Although some of the traditional stereotypes may be fading, present-day Greeks still place a high premium on family values and maintain close ties with parents, siblings, and the extended family, which may include grandparents, aunts, uncles, and godparents. Famous for their sense of hospitality, Greeks will often put their guests' needs before their own.

Above: **In Greece's rugged terrain, donkeys have been the favorite means of transportation for centuries.**

Opposite: **Young couples in traditional Greek costume.**

55

Tantalus delicatessen, a Greek delicatessen in New York City run by the descendants of Greek immigrants.

POPULATION TRENDS

Greece has a population of 10.6 million. Most of the population lives on the Greek peninsula; the islands are sparsely populated. The population growth rate in Greece is a low 0.2 percent per year.

After the military junta was overthrown in the mid-1970s, Greeks living in the countryside began migrating to the cities looking for work. As a result, almost half of the present-day population is concentrated in Greater Athens and Thessaloníki. Twenty percent of rural Greeks work as farmers in the countryside.

From the late 1800s to the end of World War II, great numbers of Greeks migrated to North America and Australia. Emigration was mainly driven by war, unemployment, and famine. It is estimated that since 1945, 2 million Greeks have moved to Australia and 2 million to the United States.

After Greece joined the EC, Greeks began migrating to Germany and Belgium in search of work. Many, however, have been forced to return to Greece after demand for immigrant labor in these countries declined.

MINORITY GROUPS

During the course of its long history, Greece has been settled by different peoples and empires: Roman, Frankish, Venetian, Byzantine, and Ottoman Turk. Although the present-day population is overwhelmingly ethnic Greek, the ethnic minorities that make up 2 percent of the population are descendants of the early rulers or recent immigrants from Slavic countries.

The minority groups are scattered around the country; some of them have preserved their own language and traditions.

A mosque stands facing the Hania harbor in Crete. Greece's Muslim population is mostly of Turkish descent.

TURKS Most of the Turks in Greece live in Thrace, the northeastern province of Greece along the border with Turkey. Many villages in Thrace have Turkish majorities, and the local governments are run by Muslim officials. The Turkish community in this region numbers 100,000 people.

In 1923, after a Greek invasion to take over Smyrna, a Turkish city with a large ethnic Greek population, led to bloody fighting between the countries, Greece and Turkey conducted a brutal population exchange. About 400,000 Turks living in Greece were deported to Turkey, and nearly 1.3 million Greeks were forced out of their homes and marched to Greece, straining the country's resources. However, some Turks living in Thrace were able to remain in Greece.

Despite ongoing friction between Turkey and Greece, especially over Cyprus, the inhabitants of Thrace live together peacefully. Turkish children attend schools where the language of instruction is Turkish. Several Turkish language newspapers are also published in Thrace.

Many Vlachs in Greece work as shepherds. Shepherds are recognizable by the crook and staff that they use to herd their sheep.

VLACHS Greek villagers use the word *Vlach* to mean "shepherds." Since the Aromani and Koutsovlach ethnic minorities have traditionally worked as shepherds, they are called Vlachs. The Vlachs, who number 100,000, speak a Romanian dialect and are believed to have come from Romania. They worship in the Greek Orthodox Church.

Another group of shepherds, the Sarakatsani, are often mistaken for Vlachs. The Sarakatsani speak only Greek and have a different set of values and social structure from the Vlachs. Nevertheless, as the groups engage in the same trade, they are in constant competition for grazing land.

ALBANIANS Many Albanians migrated to Greece in the 14th century. Most of them have assimilated into Greek society. Since 1991, a new wave of Albanian immigrants has come to Greece to work, mostly illegally. It is estimated that there are between 300,000 to 400,000 recent Albanian immigrants living in Greece today. They have faced difficulties and have endured discriminatory treatment by the Greek authorities and the media.

JEWS Jews have lived in Greece since before the time of Christ. In the 13th century, Jewish immigrants from Italy, France, Germany, and Poland settled in Thessaloníki. The greatest influx, however, came in the 15th century, when Sephardic Jews, expelled from Spain during the Inquisition, settled in Greece, where there was religious tolerance under Turkish Muslim rule.

During the Nazi occupation of Greece in World War II, most Jews were taken to concentration camps across Europe. The Jewish population in Greece fell sharply from 78,000 to less than 13,000 at the end of the war.

Greek Jews today are mainly merchants or professionals. Thessaloníki is still a center of Jewish intellectual and commercial life, but the majority of Greek Jews live in Athens.

Most minority groups have assimilated into Greek society.

SLAVS There are two Slavic groups in Greece—the Slavs from Macedonia and the Pomaks from Thrace. Although they have lived in Greece for centuries, Macedonian Slavs continue to speak Slavic languages. The Bulgarian-speaking Pomaks are Muslims who did not migrate to Turkey in the 1920s. The Slavs in Greece are estimated to number about 60,000.

A Greek middle-class family shops in Crete.

SOCIAL DIVISIONS

There are no strict class divisions in Greece. Generally, Greeks are able to climb up the social ladder through higher education or property ownership.

In villages, the lowest level of society is made up of landless farm laborers. The middle classes are small farm owners, merchants, and skilled workers. Prosperous farm owners, large shopkeepers, successful merchants, professionals, and government officials make up the upper level.

In towns, the lowest class owns no property, has little education and no consumer power. They are laborers, unskilled factory workers, and domestic servants. The lower-middle class consists of craftsmen, small shopkeepers, traders, and civil servants. The upper-middle class includes professionals, business people, and senior government officials. Urban upper classes include mercantile ship owners, bankers, and industrialists.

FOLK DRESS

Each province in Greece boasts its own traditional clothing. Greeks wear these outfits on special and festive occasions. Although the clothing of each province will reflect a pattern and style from a particular period in Greek history, they generally have one thing in common—the fabric contains exquisite and elaborate embroidery. Greek women have excelled at embroidery for centuries.

Folk dress for women consists of colorful skirts and embroidered vests. An important item in women's folk dress is the colorful scarf worn on the head. Necklaces, earrings, and bracelets add richness to women's dress.

A popular folk outfit for men is the *foustanella* ("foos-tah-NEL-lah"), a pleaded white skirt, which is worn by the *evzones*, the guards of the presidential residence and the parliament. During ceremonial occasions, they wear a white shirt and a *foustanella*, an embroidered dark blue jacket, white stockings, and red shoes with pompoms on the toes. A hat tops the whole outfit.

Traditional folk dress for Greek women is characterized by elaborate and colorful head scarves.

LIFESTYLE

GREEKS EMBRACE HELLENISM, an ideology based on the ideals that were regarded as exceptional and glorious in ancient Greece. All Greeks, regardless of background, occupation, or region, are aware of the tremendous role their ancestors have played in the development of Western civilization.

During the years of Turkish rule, Greeks relied on Hellenism to retain their identity. This ideology lives on today, as modern Greeks strive to follow in their ancestors' footsteps by contributing their knowledge and cultural heritage to global society.

THE FAMILY

The typical household in Greece consists of a husband, wife, children, and grandparents. Unmarried adults rarely leave their parents' home to live on their own, and in some regions, it is the custom for married children to live with their parents until they have established their own households.

Traditionally, a rural newlywed couple lives in the home of the groom's parents or in a home his parents provide for them in the village. If labor is needed for the family farm, married children may continue to live with their parents indefinitely. On some of the islands, a married couple lives in the wife's village, and often, her family provides the home as part of the traditional wedding gift.

Family members in Greece work together to preserve the family property. In poorer families with no property, the sons contribute their wages. A Greek considers it a special duty to take care of his or her parents for as long as they live, so it is natural for elderly parents to move in with their married children after they have established independent households. As a result, few senior citizens live alone or in homes for the elderly.

Greek society has some important unifying factors that make all Greeks feel as one people—a glorious heritage, a common religion and sense of values, and a popular tongue.

Opposite: **A modern city center in Crete. The 20th century has brought much economic change to Greece.**

SPECIAL RELATIONSHIPS

KOUMBAROS/KOUMBARA In Greece, a special bond exists between families that are not related. This relationship is based on the tradition of choosing a *koumbaros* ("koom-BAH-rohs") or a *koumbara* ("koom-BAH-rah"), a family friend who acts as the best man or the maid of honor at a wedding. Often, they will also be asked to be the godparent of the couple's first child. As such, the *koumbaros* or the *koumbara* becomes a spiritual member of the family.

Although it is an artificially created kinship, religious law prohibits marriage between the children and godchildren of a *koumbaros,* because the relationship between the family and the *koumbaros* is considered as close as that of blood relations.

PATRIDA A Greek's homeland is his or her *patrida* ("pah-TREE-dah"). Over the last two hundred years, millions of Greeks have left their country to start new lives in faraway countries such as the United States and Australia. However, Greeks remain extremely devoted to their homeland. It is not unusual for Greeks living overseas to show their patriotism by flying the Greek flag on their homes and businesses on Greek Independence Day.

PATRONAGE Greeks are intensely loyal to people in the family but traditionally distrustful of people who are not their relatives. In addition, a long history of unstable governments has led Greeks to feel that the only people they can truly rely on are family members and relatives. Government and public officials, in general, are regarded with hostility.

This widespread belief has created a heavy reliance on patrons, people of high political standing who look after others in exchange for allegiance. This give-and-take relationship serves both the patron and the benefactor equally and often lasts a lifetime. For example, besides pledging political support, a fisherman may offer a weekly gift of fish to the patron in return for speeding up a bureaucratic procedure.

Above: **Greek men gather at a café to enjoy a drink and companionship.**

Opposite: **Greek children are often doted on by their grandparents.**

PHILOXENIA Hospitality, or *philoxenia* ("fil-lox-eh-NEE-ah"), is an old Greek tradition. Some say it began in Homeric times as a sacred duty; others feel that the harshness of the Greek landscape may have caused Greeks to be kind to anyone in need of food or shelter.

Whatever its origin, it is clear that the stranger benefits from the consideration that Greeks have for the wants and needs of others. Greeks judge themselves by the extent of their hospitality. If they fail in their duty to put their guests' needs before their own, they will have damaged the honor of not only their ancestors, but of the community as a whole.

GREEK WOMEN

In rural Greek households, it is the duty of the women to look after the home and family while the men go out to work.

In the rural areas and villages of Greece, men and women still hold traditional roles. Marriage and family make up the main focus of life for Greek women, and many in the older generation measure their worth by their accomplishments as mothers and homemakers. The men are expected by society to be responsible for providing food and shelter for the family.

In the cities, the traditional attitude about the role of the sexes is less evident than in the rural areas. Traditional beliefs about these roles have increasingly been eroded by urbanization. More women are entering the workforce and earning their own living. As a result, women have a greater sense of independence. The double-income family, where both marriage partners work and contribute to household expenses, is also becoming increasingly common in Greece today.

Many of the gains made by Greek women were achieved only in the years after World War II. Women first won equal voting rights in 1952. The following year, the first women were elected to Greece's parliament. By 1977 women made up 38.7 percent of all university students in Greece; by 1980, 9.5 percent of the country's army and 5 percent of the navy consisted of women. By 2000 women made up 40 percent of the Greek workforce and 60 percent of university graduates. However, regardless of the fact that women enjoy equal rights with men before the law, women earn only about 80 percent of a man's wages for performing the same job.

The year 1983 was a landmark for women's rights in Greece. The country's new Family Law came into force, making the spouses equal in decision making. It gave women the right to keep their birth names after

Minister of Culture from 1981 to 1989, and from 1993 to 1994, Melina Mercouri (1925–94), a former actress, started a campaign to ask the British government to return the Parthenon marbles to Greece.

marriage, legalized divorce by mutual consent, and abolished a married woman's need to get her husband's permission to conduct business, remove her children from the city, or put them in a school.

In 1981 film actress Melina Mercouri became the country's first woman minister of culture, a post she was to hold for eight years. Her tenure is noted for her battle to get the British to return the Parthenon marbles, carvings and statues that were taken from the country and sent to Britain in the early 19th century.

In 1992, at the summer Olympic Games in Barcelona, Paraskevi Patoulidou won the 100-m hurdles, becoming the first Greek track-and-field medalist since the first modern Olympics began in 1896. Ekaterini Thanou followed in her footsteps by securing a silver medal in the same category at the 2000 Olympic Games in Sydney.

Former Member of Parliament Dora Bakoyiannis, a member of the New Democracy Party, became the first woman mayor of Athens when she won the municipal elections held in October 2002. She will be the first woman ever to be mayor of a city hosting the Olympic Games.

Obviously, the days when Greek dramatist Euripides wrote, "a woman should be everything in the house and nothing outside it" are long past!

Greek schoolchildren are taught the history of a beautiful Classical sculpture at the National Archaeological Museum in Athens.

PHILOTIMO

Philotimo ("feel-LOH-tih-moh") is a word that describes the feeling of honor that is ingrained in the daily behavior of many Greeks. *Philotimo* involves gaining the respect of others for oneself and one's family by upholding the family honor. Young children in Greece are taught from an early age to avoid losing face in public, as it would be a disgrace to the family honor.

Philotimo is important at all levels of society. Family honor is so sacred that, until recently, a typical defense in many murder cases was that the crime had been committed to uphold the family honor.

EDUCATION

Greeks value formal education greatly, as it is considered an essential requirement for improving one's status in society.

The Greek education system has undergone reform in the last 30 years to become more accessible to all members of society and offer more practical courses. As a result, the literacy rate has risen from just 30 percent in the 1950s to 95 percent in the 1990s.

Public education in Greece is compulsory and free. All children aged 6 to 12 must attend *dimotiko* ("dee-moh-tee-KOH"), or elementary school. Three years of *gymnasio* ("gee-MNAH-see-oh"), or middle school, follows *dimotiko*. *Lykio* ("LEE-kee-oh"), or high school, is not mandatory but most students do attend, graduating after three years. After high school, students take examinations to enter a university or a technical school.

Greek men enjoy a chat over a cup of coffee in a *kafeneíon* supportive of the PASOK party.

AMONG FRIENDS

Greeks love to socialize and spend time with friends. During warm weather months, families go out every night and many take long walks on Sunday afternoons. Families visit other families, and parents sit on benches while the children run around the village square and play.

Greeks love to talk—they love poetry, arguing about politics, and word play. They would rather pass time at a crowded beach or park than take a short trip to get some peace and quiet.

After an evening jaunt, elderly men often stop at the local *kafeneíon* ("kah-fay-NEE-on"), or café. A traditional *kafeneíon* is almost exclusively patronized by men. Greek men enjoy discussing world events with their friends over a cup of coffee or a glass of wine. Political alliances also play a part in the life of a *kafeneíon*, as supporters of a political party may gather at one *kafeneíon*, while supporters of a rival party gather at another place.

A *kafeneíon* is no place for the younger generation, who prefer outdoor recreation, clubbing, and dancing.

WORRY BEADS

A traditional pastime for Greek men in a *kafeneíon* is to click away at their worry beads. The beads (*below*) range from plastic to silver to mother-of-pearl and are strung on thread and held in the hand. The clicking sound that is made as the fingers "count" the beads creates a type of background music that accompanies lively conversations in many *kafeneíons*.

Greek men have been using these beads for centuries. Contrary to their name, worry beads, or *komboloi* ("kohm-boh-LOY"), have little to do with worry. In fact, they are said to lessen tension, and the use of these beads is said to be the oldest and simplest way to relieve stress.

Worry beads may have been first used in India by Hindus and Buddhists as prayer beads. Later, Muslims also began using them as prayer beads, often with 99 beads per string to honor the number of ways Allah is glorified. The Greeks may have adopted the use of worry beads from the Turks, who are Muslim.

Roman Catholic countries in Europe also have a tradition of using rosary beads to count prayers. In Greece, however, the use of these beads never achieved any religious significance; rather it evolved into a secular pastime practiced by older men.

A Greek couple on a rented scooter spend a holiday in Crete.

LOVE IS IN THE AIR

In traditional Greek society, single people did not choose whom they would marry; this was arranged by the parents of the young couple.

Such matrimonial matchmaking is increasingly rare in modern society, especially in the cities. Nevertheless, parental approval is still very important to young people, and few will go against their parents' wishes should they voice strong objections to a prospective partner.

Until the 1960s, young unmarried women in Greece dressed and behaved very modestly. A young woman's demure appearance was regarded as a symbol of the family honor. Women could not spend time alone with a man until they were formally engaged, as any hint of flirtation on the woman's part could damage her reputation and the family honor.

Present-day Greek women living in the cities, however, dress in the latest fashion from Western Europe and North America, which do not always conform to the traditional principles. Young men and women might meet while traveling, through the Internet, at the beach, or at clubs.

TYING THE KNOT

Civil marriages have been legal since 1982, but most Greek couples see a church ceremony as the only valid contract. Traditionally, the wedding ceremony in a Greek Orthodox church symbolizes the formation of the family. Although the Greek Orthodox wedding ceremony does not include the exchange of vows, it is nevertheless filled with rites that symbolize the unity of husband and wife in a sacred bond.

Greek families are characterized by close-knit relationships, big family feasts for every important occasion, and the presence of a strong matriarchal figure. A traditional Greek family is usually big, including

Marriage is always a family affair in Greece and would not be complete without a big reunion and celebration.

An upper-class Greek home in Crete.

grandparents and many children, but modern society has affected the structure of the Greek family.

Today, children go abroad or to the cities to study; young couples prefer to have only one or two children; and with most women pursuing a career, household chores and responsibilities are increasingly being shared by the couple. Traditionally seen as an affront to the family honor, divorces in Greece have increased dramatically since the 1960s. However, Greece has one of the lowest divorce rates in the EU.

The dowry was an honored tradition in Greek marriages. Women used to enter marriage with a sum of money or a piece of property given to the couple by her parents. The dowry was meant to help the young couple establish their first home but also gave the parents some authority over the decisions made by the newlywed couple.

The dowry is now illegal. Young urban Greek couples prefer to live their lives independent of their parents. However, the tradition is still practiced to a certain extent in the countryside.

An infant baptism at a Greek Orthodox church.

CHILDREN

Greeks love children, often seeing them as a necessary fulfillment of marriage. In traditional society, *philotimo* is associated with having children.

Traditionally, manhood depended, in part, on the ability to produce a son, although having a daughter was considered better than remaining childless. For the woman, the ideal was to become a mother and educate her children to uphold the family and community values.

The birth of a child is a major event, especially if it is the first child. The rites leading to adulthood begin with baptism. A child receives his or her religious and regional identity when his or her name is pronounced in the presence of the priest, godparents, and parents.

A *chrisma* ("CHRIS-mah"), or confirmation ceremony, follows the baptism. The child's forehead, eyes, hands, and feet are anointed with special myrrh from the Patriarchate of Constantinople, thus marking his or her official membership into the Greek Orthodox Church.

In the first four years of life, Greek children are indulged by both parents. By age 6, Greek children are considered responsible family members who also contribute to keeping the family honor. As they grow up, they become more aware of *philotimo* to ensure that they will have the respect of others.

Greek parents pay a lot of attention to the development of their children's language abilities. Because the ability to communicate is such a valued social skill, parents make sure that their children will be able to entertain, argue, and convince by means of language. This talent is also essential for maintaining self-esteem.

DEATH RITUALS

Death rituals in Greece are marked by mourners in black during funerals and memorial services. After the church service, a procession of family and friends makes its way along the streets to the cemetery, where a shorter service is held before the internment of the coffin. The dead are always buried, as the Greek Orthodox Church forbids cremation.

The most important memorial services take place 40 days after death and again on the fifth-year anniversary of the death. A standard part of the fifth-year memorial is to exhume the body to remove the bones. The bones are first washed with wine, then placed in an ossuary, which is a depository for the bones of the dead. This is done in part to relieve the shortage of land in Greek cemeteries.

Rituals that mark transitions from one stage of life to another are considered by Greeks to be similar in nature. For example, mourning songs and wedding songs are much the same, and it is common for young unmarried people to be buried in white clothes.

A typical Greek burial ground next to the church.

RELIGION

THE OFFICIAL RELIGION OF GREECE is Greek Orthodox Christianity, an autonomous faction of the Eastern Orthodox Church. While there is tolerance for other religions, the constitution refers to Greek Orthodox Christianity as the official religion, and proselytizing, or trying to convert people to a different religion, by other religious groups is forbidden.

About 98 percent of Greeks are members of the Greek Orthodox Church. The Orthodox Church has about 150 million members worldwide, of whom 10 million are within Greece. Of the remaining 2 percent of the Greek population, 1.3 percent are Muslim, and 0.7 percent are Jewish, Protestant, or Roman Catholic.

CHRISTIAN BEGINNINGS

Christianity was brought to Greece at the beginning of the first century by the apostle Paul. But it was not until A.D. 313, when Emperor Constantine was converted after seeing a vision of a cross in the sky, that Christianity became the official religion of the Roman empire.

Constantine moved the capital from Rome to Byzantium, later renamed Constantinople, in present-day Turkey. Geographical, cultural, and linguistic differences between the two capitals led to a bitter rivalry between the bishop of Constantinople, called the patriarch, and the pope in Rome.

Both sides disagreed sharply on the issue of who had final authority over matters of faith. The pope insisted that he had absolute power over the entire church, while the patriarch held firm that decisions on matters of faith must be made by a council. They also disagreed on the issue of celibacy for priests. In 1054 the patriarch and the pope excommunicated one another, marking the separation of the Christian church. From that time on, the patriarch of Constantinople represented the Eastern Orthodox Church, and the pope headed the Roman Catholic Church.

Religion is, for historical reasons, considered to be part of Greek culture. The Greeks' firm religious beliefs are reflected in the altars and facades of many Greek homes.

Opposite: **The bell tower of a Greek Orthodox church overlooks the sea in the island of Santorini.**

77

The Byzantine monastery of Dafni was founded in the fifth century.

CHURCH AUTHORITIES

Eastern Orthodox Church beliefs and practices have remained unchanged since the first millennium. The word "orthodox," in fact, is derived from a Greek word that means "correct belief," emphasizing that the religion is devoted to the original faith of the first apostles.

After Greece became independent from the Ottoman Empire, the Greek Orthodox Church gained independence from Eastern Orthodox patriarchal authority. The Greek Orthodox Church is currently governed by the Holy Synod, a body consisting of all Greek Orthodox bishops. The synod meets once a year under the chairmanship of the Archbishop of Athens and All Greece to discuss matters concerning the church.

The Greek Orthodox Church has no figure comparable to the pope. The Ecumenical Patriarch of Istanbul, formerly known as the Patriarch of Constantinople, is the patriarch and spiritual leader of all the Orthodox churches. Unlike the pope, however, he is not considered infallible, as ancient Christian belief emphasized the equality of all bishops.

RELIGIOUS PRACTICES

For centuries, religion has been closely associated with Greek nationalism. During the years of Turkish rule, the Church was the one institution that united all Greeks. The Patriarch of Constantinople maintained both spiritual and civil powers over the Greek population, while monks and village priests held secret classes to preserve the Greek language and the Orthodox faith among Greeks. Churches soon became sanctuaries dedicated to the preservation of Greek culture and faith.

Although most of the Greek population is affiliated to the church and all the important ceremonies in a Greek's life, such as baptism, marriage, and the funeral, are held in church, many Greeks do not attend church regularly. However, their faith is evident in their day-to-day activities.

Candles and decorated icons in a church on Good Friday.

Most Greek families devote a corner of their home to a display of icons, religious paintings, along with lamps and holy oil. In times of trouble, Greeks sometimes go to church to seek divine intervention by lighting and placing a candle at the foot of the image of a famous saint.

The most important festivals in the Greek calendar are based on Christian events, such as Easter and Epiphany. Even secular events such as the harvest or the return of a fishing fleet from the sea are celebrated by small religious ceremonies. Priests may also be asked to bless the opening of a new shop or building of a new house. Patron saint's days are more important celebrations than birthdays.

Religion is a strong unifying factor in the countryside. Local churches are often the focus of a community and all projects concerning the church are a means of drawing villagers together to work for a common cause.

FROM MOUNT OLYMPUS: RELIGION IN ANCIENT GREECE

Ancient peoples throughout the world have tried to make sense of the natural world by attributing natural phenomena, such as rain, thunder, and earthquakes, to the work of gods and goddesses. Scandinavian, Chinese, Indian, and Egyptian mythologies have gods whose exploits reflect the character of the people. The Greeks also had their own pantheon of gods, and the colorful stories created around them have influenced European thought and culture since ancient times. Many stories or myths about the Greek gods originated as early as 700 B.C.

Myths of the gods were passed down from generation to generation through storytelling and poetry and have been preserved through the ages in the works of the classical Greek writers. Homer's *The Iliad* and *The Odyssey*, and Hesiod's *Theogony* incorporate most of the characters and themes of classical Greek mythology.

Theogony describes the origin and history of the gods. According to this work, the universe was formed from an empty and shapeless mass called Chaos. From Chaos sprang Gaea, or Earth, who gave birth to Uranus, or Heaven. Gaea and Uranus, as rulers of the universe, gave birth to the Titans. Two of the Titans, Cronus and Rhea, had six children. Their children became the Olympian gods Demeter, Hades, Hera, Hestia, Poseidon, and Zeus. Other Olympian gods were Aphrodite, Apollo, Ares, Artemis, Athena (*right*), Hermes, and Hephaestus.

The Olympian gods were thought to dwell in the sky or on Mount Olympus in Thessaly, thus their name. Earthbound gods were believed to live on or under the earth. Leading the ranks of gods was Zeus, the father of the gods. Hera, his wife, was the queen of the heavens and the goddess of marriage. Among Zeus's brothers and sisters were Poseidon, god of the sea, and Hestia, goddess of hearth and home.

Zeus had many children who were also gods. Hephaestus was the god of fire; Athena was the goddess of wisdom; Apollo (*right*) was the god of the sun, music, and poetry; Artemis was the goddess of wildlife and the moon; Ares was the god of war; Aphrodite was the goddess of love; Hermes was the gods' messenger to humans and later god of science and invention; and Dionysus was the god of wine and drama.

Because each god or goddess ruled over some part of the world and the lives of humans, ancient Greeks worshiped those who could influence their everyday needs. For example, Poseidon, god of the waters, could oversee a successful voyage; Athena, with her wisdom, could help a person solve a problem.

There were also lesser beings, such as the nymphs, who guarded nature, and the Fates, who controlled the destiny of all humans. There were also nine

muses, goddesses who provided inspiration for the arts and sciences. Calliope was the muse of epic poetry; Clio, the muse of history; Erato, the muse of lyric poetry; Euterpe, the muse of music; Melpomene, the muse of tragedy; Polymnia, the muse of sacred poetry; Terpsichore, the muse of dance and song; Thalia, the muse of comedy; and Urania, the muse of astronomy.

Roman mythology is nearly identical to that of the Greeks. The Romans greatly admired Greek civilization, so they adopted many Greek gods as their own and gave them Roman names: Zeus was called Jupiter; Poseidon was called Neptune; Dionysus was called Bacchus; Aphrodite was called Venus; and Hermes was called Mercury.

Greek Orthodox priests wear black robes and distinctive hats.

WEARING THE ROBES

In contrast to the Roman Catholic clergy, Eastern Orthodox priests can be married, provided that they are married before ordination. Once a man has been ordained, he may not marry. If a married priest becomes a widower, he is not allowed to remarry. Only unmarried and celibate priests are eligible to become bishops; married priests cannot become bishops.

Since married priests cannot rise to higher office, married men who decide to become priests receive only two years of theological training rather than higher religious education.

Rural priests are often men of little schooling who receive small salaries from the government. In order to support their families, rural priests usually must farm or work the land, just like the other villagers. Although he is respected for his special duties and obligations, the villagers do not hold the local priest in awe. Rural priests are regarded as family men who must provide for their families in the same way as other village men.

Greek Orthodox clergymen wear flowing black robes and black rimless hats. For the church service, colorful brocade vestments are added. Traditionally the clergy did not shave or cut their hair, which was tied in a coiled knot at the base of their necks.

MONASTIC LIFE

Monasteries play an important role in the Greek Orthodox Church. Even before the arrival of Christianity in Greece, Greeks went to monasteries to practice spiritual discipline, spending the day in prayer and meditation. Unlike their counterparts in the Roman Catholic Church, Orthodox monks are often laymen, which means they are not part of the clergy.

Mount Athos, near Thessaloníki, is famous for its many monasteries, some dating back to the 10th century. This religious haven has been granted semiautonomous status from Greece. Only men are allowed to visit the area.

Throughout the 1,000-year history of Greek monasteries, the numbers of monks has fluctuated from high to low. Surprisingly, in the last 30 years, there has been a resurgence in interest among young men in leading a spiritual life. More than 1,000 monks currently live on historic Mount Athos.

There are three types of Greek Orthodox monks. The cenobitic monks live in a community and share meals, property, services, and work. Idiorrhythmic monks live in small settlements and pray according to their own schedule, only coming together with other monks on feast days and Sundays. Anchorites are monks who live in remote places as hermits.

Greece's monasteries are located in remote places, such as Pindus mountains of Thessaly.

Monasteries in Greece range from beautiful and charming cloisters to inaccessible and isolated retreats, such as the Meteora monasteries located on rare rock formations in a valley near the Pindus mountains.

Going home after the Sunday morning service.

SUNDAY AT CHURCH

A Sunday service at a Greek Orthodox church can last up to three hours. In traditional churches, men and women sit on separate sides of the church. Children gather near a platform close to the front of the church. People may sit on the pews or stand.

Unlike in Roman Catholic churches, there are no statues of Christ and the saints in Eastern Orthodox churches. Instead there are beautiful icons, portraits of saints, which play an important part in the Orthodox faith. Icons are traditional religious pictures painted on wooden panels or made in mosaic or enamel. On entering a church, worshipers traditionally kiss the icon of Christ first, then the icon of the Virgin Mary, and then the icons of the saints.

Although it may seem that Eastern Orthodox believers worship the images of Christ and the Virgin Mary found in every Orthodox church, the Eastern Orthodox Church rejects idolatry. Icons are not worshiped but are thought to be an opening between heaven and earth through which those in heaven reveal themselves. Because of this, it is essential that the image on the icons match all previous images of a saint. Thus most icons bear similar features that do not follow the rules of realistic art but those of a symbolic spiritual representation.

Creating icons is a holy task, often undertaken by several monks, each of whom specializes in a particular part, such as the hand or the face.

SUPERSTITIONS

Although Christianity replaced the pagan faiths of the Greeks nearly 1,700 years ago, some remnants of the ancient beliefs have survived. Many of these superstitions do not follow the teachings of the Church. Crucifixes and charms in the form of eyes (*right*) are believed to ward off the "evil eye," bad luck that is the result of other people's jealous stares.

Instead of medical doctors, magic healers are sometimes called upon to treat the sick. It is estimated that there are more than 15,000 professional astrologers and fortune-tellers in Greece.

Sacrificial animal offerings still take place. In Gouménissa, a village near Thessaloníki, the tradition of sacrificing a calf continues yearly at a wayside chapel, and the occasion is celebrated with folk dancing and feasting.

THE *ANASTENARIA* ("ah-nahs-teh-NAH-ree-ah") are rituals of firewalking and spirit possession that take place in the Macedonian villages of Aghia Eleni and Langadhás. These rites are performed by Kostilides, a group of people from eastern Thrace who settled in Macedonia in the 1920s. The rites, however, may have started as early as 1250, when a group of Thracian villagers rescued icons from a burning church.

The *Anastenaria* begin on May 21, when the Greek Orthodox Church celebrates the festivals of St. Constantine and his mother, St. Helen (Eleni). Dancers hold on to icons of these two saints as they make their way across burning coals. St. Constantine is believed to possess the firewalking dancers and protect them from harm as they step on the hot coals. At the beginning, the dance is one of suffering, but it transforms into one of joy.

Anastenaria firewalkers claim to feel warmth, but no pain. After leaving the fire, the participants feel they have acted according to the will of the saint. Before the fire dance, a calf is sacrificed. The celebrations last through May 23.

Anastenaria rites are not recognized by the Greek Orthodox Church, which regards the dancers as heathens. Firewalkers have been excommunicated by the Church.

LANGUAGE

GREEK, THE OFFICIAL LANGUAGE of Greece, has been spoken for more than 3,000 years, making it the oldest language in Europe. When other European societies had not yet developed a written language, the Greeks were cultivating a rich literary tradition.

Greece is linguistically homogeneous, as most of the population speaks Greek. Minority groups in Greece, which account for 2 percent of the population, speak their own languages—a Romanian dialect called Vlach, Turkish, Slav, Albanian, or Pomak, a Bulgarian dialect—in addition to Greek.

ORIGINS

Modern Greek is a direct descendant of the Proto-Indo-European language, which was spoken centuries before Christ by civilizations on the Aegean islands, the Greek mainland, and in Asia Minor. Proto-Indo-European is the same language family from which many European languages are derived, but Greek does not bear any close affiliation with other languages in the family because it evolved through the centuries in relative isolation. Unlike other isolated languages, however, Greek continues to be spoken today, and early written records of ancient Greek still exist.

The Greek language is believed to be one of the most sophisticated languages ever devised. In fact, Greek is the language of choice for a number of scholars and poets of many nationalities because they feel that no other language can so adequately convey meaning and beauty.

Above: **A bilingual sign at the entrance of an ancient Greek monastery is written in English and Greek.**

Opposite: **Two Greeks say a quick hello under the signboard of a shop.**

THE ALPHABET

The Greek alphabet consists of 24 letters and at first glance may look intimidating to those unfamiliar with it, but it is actually much simpler to learn than the English alphabet. The pronunciation rules for the Greek alphabet are regular and, therefore, easier to master. Because alphabets ideally attempt to indicate separate sounds by separate symbols, it may be said that Greek has an ideal alphabet. In fact, the word "alphabet" is based on the first two letters of the Greek alphabet—"alpha" and "beta."

In Greek, it is important to correctly stress the syllables of a word. A word pronounced with the stress on the first syllable may have an entirely different meaning from the same word with the stress on the third syllable.

The alphabets of all major European languages are to some extent based on the ancient Greek alphabet. The Roman alphabet (used to write English) is sometimes called the Western form of the Greek alphabet.

Ancient Greek writing inscribed on stone ruins.

PRONOUNCING GREEK LETTERS						
A α	alpha	'a' as in f<u>a</u>ther, <u>a</u>rm		N ν	ni	'n' as in <u>n</u>ose
B β	beta	'v' as in <u>v</u>iolent		Ξ ξ	xi	'x' as in fi<u>x</u>
Γ γ	gamma	'g' as in <u>g</u>uild		O o	omicron	'o' as in h<u>o</u>t
Δ δ	delta	'd' as in <u>d</u>emocracy		Π π	pi	'p' as in 'pie'
E ε	epsilon	'e' as in g<u>e</u>t		P ρ	rho	'r' as in <u>r</u>hinoceros
Z ζ	zeta	'z' as in <u>z</u>oo		Σ σ	sigma	's' as in <u>s</u>ignal
H η	eta	'e' as in m<u>ee</u>t		T τ	tau	't' as in <u>t</u>emple
Θ θ	theta	'th' as in theater		Υ υ	upsilon	'oo' as in r<u>u</u>de
I ι	iota	'i' as in pol<u>i</u>ce		Φ φ	phi	'ph' as in <u>ph</u>ilosophy
K κ	kappa	'k' as in <u>k</u>itten		X χ	chi	'h' as in <u>h</u>orse
Λ λ	lamda	'l' as in <u>l</u>ion, <u>l</u>amb		Ψ ψ	psi	'ps' as in eclip<u>s</u>e
M μ	mi	'm' as in <u>m</u>iss		Ω ω	omega	'o' as in <u>o</u>ral

There are over 100 daily newspapers in Greece, most of which are known for their sensationalist taste.

THE MEDIA

The Greek media exercise much influence over the population, and tend to focus on sensationalist news and articles. As most of the Greek media are owned by powerful businessmen with interests in other sectors of the economy, television and radio programs and newspaper and magazine articles are filled with information promoting certain products or services. The print media tend to concentrate on sensationalist news stories, often without regard for objective or in-depth reporting.

In the 1980s, the government gave up its monopoly over television and radio broadcasting. As a result, privately-owned television and radio stations increased dramatically in the 1990s. In 2001 the National Radio and Television Council, a government body set up to grant licenses to new, privately owned television and radio stations, gave authorization for 35 more radio stations to be created in Athens.

In 1994 the Greek government created the Ministry of Press and Information to handle media issues. The Minister of Press and Information also serves as the government spokesperson. The ministry also operates the Greek state broadcaster ERT, in addition to three television channels that broadcast nationwide and five national radio channels.

DIALECTS

A unique aspect of the Greek language is that it consists of two dialects: *dimotiki* ("dee-moh-tee-KEE") and *katharévousa* ("kah-thah-REH-voo-sah"). Historically, *dimotiki* was the language of the common people and is still used in casual speech by all Greeks. *Katharos* means "pure." In the 1830s, scholars created a "superior language," *katharévousa,* based on the classic tongue. This artificial language became the official language of Greece, and everything from laws to nursery rhymes were written in *katharévousa.* Opposition to this "dead" language was strong, however, and in 1976 *dimotiki* was declared the official language of Greece.

GREEK INFLUENCE ON THE ENGLISH LANGUAGE

English and other European languages have borrowed many words from advanced civilizations like the Greeks. In fact, Latin and Greek are quite prevalent in English. Some words derived from Greek in our vocabulary are acronym, agnostic, autocracy, chlorine, kudos, pathos, telegram, and xylophone.

Sometimes, the borrowed element is a root that serves as the basis for longer words. English has many such Greek roots. On the right are some Greek roots that, combined with other words, form words we use every day.

Root	Meaning	English words
autos	self	autograph, automatic
biblios	book	biblical, bibliography
cryptos	secret	crypt, cryptic
dynamis	power	dynamic, dynamite
graphein	writing	graphic, graphite
homos	same	homogenize, homonym
logy	study of	geology, biology
micro	small	microcosm, microbe
neos	new	neon, neolithic
orthos	right	orthodontic, orthopedic
philos	love	philanthropy, philosophy
scope	watch	telescope, microscope
tele	far	television, telephone

GESTURES

Body language and nonverbal gestures are a very important channel of communication. However, people tend to assume that these channels of communication have universal meaning. This, of course, is far from true. One delightful gesture any visitor to a Greek home will experience is to be greeted with a hug and a kiss on both cheeks.

Greeks are eager to argue about anything, but to them, arguing is more a lively pastime than a disagreement. An important part of this activity is the amount of gesticulating that accompanies discussions. Proving that the arguments are not serious, Greeks generally calm down quite quickly after a heated conversation.

Some typical body language used in Greece includes:

1. Crossed fingers, which usually signify hope or wishing for something to Americans, is the sign of two people in a close, romantic relationship.

2. A pursed hand gesture is a sign of excellence.

3. Pulling on the lower eyelid indicates superiority or disbelief.

4. The head tossed jerkily upward in a backward motion means "no."

Greeks do not wave with an open hand. In fact, it is considered an insult to show the palm of the hand with the fingers extended. Greeks wave with the palm closed. Greeks also make a puff of breath through pursed lips, as if spitting, after giving a compliment. This is a superstition meant to protect the person receiving the compliment from the "evil eye."

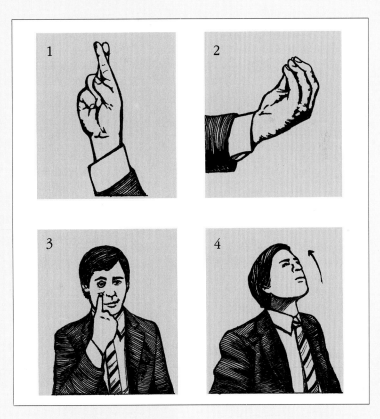

ARTS

WESTERN CIVILIZATION IS INDEBTED to Greece for its artistic legacy. In fact, most forms of Greek art, such as architecture, painting, sculpture, and literature, have had a direct influence on the development of the arts in the West.

After the Athenians defeated the Persian army in the battle of Salamis in 480 B.C., Athens became a center for democracy and the arts under the enlightened rule of Pericles. He not only rebuilt the city but also summoned the best artists and scholars in Greece to Athens. During this era, known as the Golden Age, the arts flourished.

The ancient Greeks were among the earliest to separate religion from the study of ideas and knowledge—a discipline that became known as philosophy. The philosophical writings of the Golden Age have formed the basis for intellectual writing in the West. Poetry and drama also developed during the Golden Age, with epic and lyric poetry and comic and tragic drama as the most enduring forms.

The ancient Greeks created architectural styles that became standard models of perfection for the entire Western world. Greek sculpture of the human body set the standard for the ideal aesthetic form.

Although no original Greek paintings have survived, their beauty is described in ancient writings and many surviving Roman paintings of later periods are believed to have been greatly influenced by ancient Greek painting.

Above: **An icon of Christ is painted on the ceiling of the Byzantine monastery in Dafni.**

Opposite: **A statue of ancient poetess Sappho stands near the harbor in Lésbos island, Sappho's hometown.**

93

EARLY GREEK LITERATURE

Greek literature, which dates back to the second millennium B.C., has been the most influential literary force in the Western world. From the days of the Roman empire to the present, Greek writing has influenced every literary form in Europe. The ancient Greeks wrote lyric and epic poetry, tragic and comic drama, philosophical essays and dialogues, literary letters, and critical and biographical histories that are well-known and continue to be read in schools and universities around the world.

The first significant Greek literary form was epic poetry—narrative poems that described the heroic deeds of gods and men. Homer, perhaps the greatest Greek poet, composed *The Iliad* and *The Odyssey* around 800 B.C. These poems, which emphasized the ideals of honor and bravery, greatly influenced Greek culture and education. *The Iliad* told the story of the Trojan War, and *The Odyssey* described the travels of Odysseus, a hero of the Trojan War.

Another important epic poem was the *Theogony*, written by Hesiod around 600 B.C. It told of the origin and history of the Greek gods. One other monumental work by Hesiod is *Works and Days*, describing the lives of Greek peasant farmers.

Lyric poems emerged around 650 B.C. These were much shorter than epic poems, and they generally described personal feelings rather than acts of valor. Lyric poetry was also sung to the music of the lyre. Another form of lyric poetry was the choral lyric, sung by groups and accompanied by music and dancing. Sappho, who is famous for her direct and intense language, and Pindar, author of the *Olympiads*, were the best-known lyric poets of this period.

An ancient Greek vase is decorated with a scene from Homer's *The Odyssey*. The hero, Odysseus, is tied to the mast of his ship to protect him from the Sirens, whose alluring singing would drive men to wreck their ships upon the rocks.

THE GOLDEN AGE

The 30-year period (461–431 B.C.) in which the arts, especially literature, flourished in Greece is known as the Golden Age. Drama emerged as one of the most important literary forms of this time.

Aeschylus, Euripides, and Sophocles were the three great tragic playwrights of the Golden Age. Comedy was just as popular, and the works of Aristophanes are the most famous. They reflected the spirited sense of freedom felt by the Athenians of the time and their ability to poke fun at themselves. The masterful use of the language and complexity of thought and insight are works of genius that are still enjoyed as great works of literature.

Prose replaced poetry as the leading literary form by the end of the fourth century B.C., and historical writings became popular. Herodotus, the "Father of History," recorded the cultural characteristics of the civilized world, focusing on the conflict between East and West. Another literary form arising during the Golden Age was rhetoric, which is the art of persuasive writing and speech. It was invented by the sophists, or teacher-philosophers.

The great philosopher Socrates died in 399 B.C., leaving no written works. Yet he is indirectly responsible for another influential literary invention—philosophical dialogue, based on his method of examining ideas. Socrates' teachings lived on through his students, especially through Plato, who kept a record of Socrates' lectures and founded a school in Athens. Plato's most famous pupil was Aristotle (384–322 B.C.). Aristotle contributed much to the study of philosophy, believing that "all men possess by nature the desire to know."

Statue of the great Greek dramatist Sophocles (496–405 B.C.) created at around 450 B.C.

HELLENISTIC AND BYZANTINE LITERATURE

After the establishment of the Roman empire in the second century B.C., Alexandria replaced Athens as the capital of Greek civilization. A new literary style, called pastoral poetry, had begun to develop around 200 B.C., launching the Hellenistic era of Greek art. Pastoral poetry described the beauty of nature and country life.

Prose also continued to develop. The works of Plutarch, a historian and biographer, have provided much information about this time. *Parallel Lives*, his most famous work, shows his desire for Greek culture to be preserved in the Roman world.

When Constantinople became the center of Greek culture, Christian religious poetry became the main literary form. The political climate of the Byzantine empire restricted Greek writers' artistic freedom; nevertheless, many important theological and historical writings were written at that time. These works continued to be written in the Greek language of the Classical period, which, by this time, was only understood by a select group of educated clergymen and scholars. Works written in the vernacular were limited to poetic romances and popular devotional writings, such as the lives of the saints.

The last original literary medium developed by the ancient Greeks was the novel, dating from the second and third centuries A.D. Greek novels were usually romantic stories with complicated plots. The most famous Greek novel is *Daphnis and Chloë,* written in the third century A.D.

Portrait of Plutarch (c. 46–120 A.D.) created at around 100 A.D.

ART AND ARCHITECTURE IN ANCIENT GREECE

Art in ancient Greece was closely connected with the worship of the gods. Much of the art centered on the human form, as the Greeks considered the gods have the form of perfect men and women.

Until the fourth century B.C., Greek architecture, sculpture, and painting were mainly functional. These art forms were used to commemorate athletic victories and religious events. The main role of the Greek architect of that time was to design and build temples for the deities, which were differentiated from secular dwellings by their elongated shape, at the end of which stood a large carved statue of a deity.

Decorative arts from this time were mainly found in tombs, although small ceramic sculptures and statuettes also decorated the homes of private individuals.

Most of the tools used by ancient Greek artists were hand tools, with the exception of the potter's wheel, which was run by a foot treadle.

The Temple of Aphaia was probably built during the Archaic period. Doric columns, typical of buildings in ancient Greece, are a prominent feature of the temple.

GEOMETRIC ART AND ARCHITECTURE

The Geometric period (about 1100–700 B.C.) of Greek art is characterized by the extensive use of geometric figures and other abstract forms. Small pieces of bronze and clay geometric sculpture have been found from this period, including a small statuette of Apollo. Like other pieces of this period, the statuette is an abstraction rather than a direct visual representation of the god. Geometric architecture in the form of temples can be found in Sparta, Olympia, and Crete. Only the foundations of these temples remain today.

GREEK ARCHITECTURAL STYLE

The most common architectural styles used in ancient Greece were the Doric, Ionic, and Corinthian styles. The Doric column (*below left*) was characterized by its simplicity and purity of line. The most famous Doric-style temple is the Parthenon in Athens. The Ionic column (*below center*) was developed at a later period and can be distinguished by its ornate design. Ionic-style temples can be found in Athens, Egypt, and Ephesus (modern Turkey). The Corinth column (*below right*) is the most ornate of the three architectural styles.

ARCHAIC ART AND ARCHITECTURE

The Archaic period lasted from 700 to 500 B.C. During the early Archaic period, temples built out of marble were erected on the Aegean islands. Limestone temples covered with marble were built on the mainland.

Stone monuments were also created for the temples. Human figures were carved exhibiting the archaic smile, a facial expression that was thought to be specific to humans only. Other significant artifacts from this time include vases painted with black figures and Corinthian-style vases often crowded with floral ornaments and monsters like the chimera.

In the middle of the Archaic period art drew inspiration from nature. Human forms became more lifelike. Paintings began to reflect three dimensions. Temples built during this time had six front columns and evenly-spaced columns all around the outside.

Sculpture of the middle Archaic period depicted people in action, often in scenes of battle or athletic pursuit. Beautiful vases covered in jet-black glaze and lively scenes were also common.

In the late Archaic period, a significant evolution occurred in vase painting—the emergence of the red-figure style, in which figures were preserved in the red of the clay surrounded by a black background.

The Theseion is a typical architectural example of the Archaic period. Built in the 5th century B.C. in central Athens, its front entrance displays six Doric columns.

CLASSICAL ART AND ARCHITECTURE

In the early part of the Classical period (500–323 B.C.), Greece rebuilt many of the temples damaged during the Persian Wars. Temples were built in the Doric style. An outstanding example of this architecture is the Temple of Zeus in Olympia. Sculpture of this time no longer exhibited the archaic smile; it showed expressions of both seriousness and joy and details were kept simple. Scenes portrayed the moment before or after a significant event. The original pieces of this period are lost, but many Roman artists, who greatly admired Greek art, made copies that still exist.

The middle Classical period saw the restoration of the many temples burned by the Persians, and work on rebuilding the Acropolis in Athens began. A monumental gateway to the Acropolis was created, and the Parthenon was built. These examples are Greek Classical art at its finest.

Other significant Doric works of the period are the Hephaesteion, which still stands in Athens, the Temple of Poseidon, and the Temple of Artemis. Great Ionic works include the Temple of Nike, the Eréchtheum, and the Temple of Athena.

The outstanding sculptors of the middle Classical period were Phidias, considered the sculptor of gods, and Polyclitus, who sculpted humans. Vase painting of the middle Classical period has a linear perspective that gives figures a three-dimensional appearance.

During the late Classical period, Athens lost its political supremacy, and its architecture declined. However, sculptures of that time are considered supreme examples of Classical art. Greek paintings from the fourth century B.C. no longer exist, but the first century A.D. paintings in Pompeii and Herculaneum in Italy were probably influenced by them. Unfired terracotta statuettes recovered mostly from tombs have survived to this day. They depict comic actors, fashionable women, dwarfs, and demigods.

WHAT ARE THE PARTHENON MARBLES?

Dedicated to the goddess Athena, the Parthenon was built by the architects Ictinus and Callicrates under the supervision of the sculptor Phidias. The original roof structure was decorated with three beautiful sets of sculpture—the metopes, the frieze, and the pediments—also known as the Parthenon marbles.

The metopes were individual sculptures that depicted various mythical battles. The frieze (*below*) was one long continuous sculpture that depicted the procession of Athenians to the temple during a festival in honor of the goddess Athena. The pediment statues depicted the birth of Athena and the fight between Athena and Poseidon for control of Attica.

In the early 1800s, British nobleman Thomas Bruce, Lord Elgin, had large numbers of marbles forcibly removed from the Parthenon with permission from the Turkish government that ruled Greece at the time. In 1816 Lord Elgin sold the sculptures to the British Museum. Thus, of the original 92 metopes, 39 are in Athens and 15 are in the British Museum. There were originally 115 panels in the frieze; 94 panels still exist, either intact or broken. Of these, 36 are in Athens, 56 are in the British Museum, and one is in the Louvre in France.

The Greek government, under a forceful initiative started by Melina Mercouri, the former Minister of Culture, has requested the return of the Parthenon marbles from the British Museum to their rightful home in Athens. If returned, the sculptures will be reunited in one collection, in a museum at the foot of the Acropolis Hill. However, the British have refused to return them.

A relief from the Hellenistic period. The ornate style shows evidence of Asian influence.

HELLENISTIC AND BYZANTINE ART

After the conquests of Alexander the Great, Greek art and architecture came under the influence of Asian arts. The arch and the vault were architectural elements introduced to Hellenistic buildings from Asia.

Small temples continued to be built Doric-style, although columns were usually in the Corinthian style. Gymnasiums, theaters, and public houses were built with great ornamentation. Private homes evolved from a rectangular hall to a rectangle built around a courtyard with columns.

Sculpture of the Hellenistic period changed from simple forms that focused the viewer's attention on one figure, to open forms that carried the eye of the viewer beyond the space occupied by the figure.

Byzantine art, which succeeded the Hellenistic period, left a legacy of important works of painting, mostly religious icons, and polyphonic chants sung in churches.

MODERN LITERATURE

During the 400 years of Turkish occupation, Greek literature stagnated. Only in areas like the Ionian islands, which never came under Ottoman rule, and Crete, Cyprus, and Rhodes, which were independent at times, did Greek literature continue to develop.

After independence in the 1830s, Greek scholars were divided about whether to use the popular spoken form of Greek (*dimotiki*) or the classical form (*katharévousa*) as the country's official language.

Katharévousa was chosen as the official language, but the demotic form of writing gained widespread support in the 20th century. After World War II, Greek literature gained international recognition due to the works of Constantine Cavafy (1863–1933), George Seferis (1900–71), who won the Nobel Prize in 1963, and Odysseus Elytis (1911–96), who won the Nobel Prize in 1979. Perhaps the best-known Greek writer is Nikos Kazantzakis (1883–1997), author of the novels *Zorba the Greek* and *The Last Temptation of Christ*. Women writers include Lydia Stephanou and Nana Issaia.

A scene from Homer's *The Odyssey*. Here, Odysseus and his men defy the Cyclops, the mythical one-eyed giant.

Above: **Greek popular singer Nana Mouskouri.**

Opposite: **The arts of weaving and embroidery are alive in Greece. Carpets, wall-hangings, and rugs can be bought in street stalls in Greece.**

MODERN MUSIC

Greek music is the most representative cultural example of the blending of Eastern and Western cultures in Greece. When the Greeks gained independence from the Turks, their musical heritage included not only their native folk music, but also Byzantine religious music.

Greece's new leaders introduced music lessons in the schools, imported musical instruments, and organized orchestras and musical societies. Their efforts succeeded in reviving musical interest in the cities.

One popular style of folk music, called *rembetika*, developed in the late 1800s. The *rembetika* is a nostalgic ballad reminiscent of Middle Eastern music. *Rembetika* is often sung accompanied by a *bouzouki* ("boo-zoo-KEE"), a mandolin-like instrument. Because of their association with bars and nightlife, *rembetika* music clubs came under attack during the 1930s and again in the 1970s, during the military regime. *Rembetika* clubs and cafés have regained popularity and can now be found in Athens and elsewhere in Greece.

One of the greatest opera singers of the 20th century, Maria Callas, was Greek. Vangelis, Nana Mouskouri, and Yanni are contemporary Greek musicians who have an international following.

MODERN ART

Greek folk art has survived through the centuries and continues to uphold the standard that made it famous. Greek folk artists are exceptionally skillful at fabric weaving, embroidery, and leatherwork.

Pottery developed on the islands and on the southern mainland for both decorative purposes and daily use. Greek pottery is noted for its simple, graceful forms. Copper, bronze, iron, and other metals replaced pottery in northern Greece and in other areas of the country. Present-day Greek artists have created replicas of ancient vases, which are sold to tourists.

Silver and gold jewelry were made not only as accesories for women, but also as decoration for firearms, weapons, and knives. The jewels were also sewn onto special costumes. Greeks continue to practice the art of jewelry, and they also sell their creations to tourists.

The Ionian islands developed a fine school of painting because of their freedom from Turkish occupation and the influence of the great masters of Venice. Ionian paintings are mainly religious icons.

After Greek independence in the 1830s, many artists went to study in Munich; the greatest of these was sculptor Yiannoulis Halepas (1854–1938). He is best-known for his work in marble. Other modern Greek artists are landscape painters Theophilos Chatzimichael (1873–1934) and Dimitris Mytaras (1934–).

LEISURE

GREEKS SPEND MUCH OF THEIR LEISURE time outdoors because they love socializing. Social life is enjoyed out in the streets, and many return home only to sleep. It is common to see Greeks walking around the city with a group of friends. Sometimes the groups look like moving parties, as they pick up old friends along the way or meet new ones as they go along.

Greeks have a word for the feeling of joy that they experience when they are sitting among friends, enjoying food, wine, or coffee, and having a good time. The feeling is called *kéfi* ("KEH-fee"). When Greeks feel *kéfi,* they may spontaneously get up and dance.

FOLK MUSIC

Greece's musical tradition is in its folk songs. Folk music is one of the few art forms that continued to develop under Turkish rule. Regional songs evolved from matters that affected the everyday lives of people.

Klephtica ("KLEF-tee-kah") are ballads that were sung by mountain folk that told of battles, heroic deeds, and defeats. Music played by the islanders, on the other hand, was smooth and disarming. The songs of those living in the valleys and plains told of enslaved people and their struggle for independence.

Greek folk songs mark every occasion—weddings, funerals, bedtime. Byzantine chants, often the only type of music heard by the Greeks during the years of Turkish rule, had a great influence on folk music. Despite the onslaught of pop music, folk songs remain an integral part of present-day Greek life.

Above: **The *bouzoúki* is used to accompany nostalgic Greek folk songs known as *rembétika* .**

Opposite: **Greece's idyllic beaches are ideal for swimming and sunbathing.**

Greek men in *foustanelles* ("foo-stah-NEH-lehs") perform a folk dance in a café.

FOLK DANCING

Dancing has played a vital role in Greek life since ancient times. Archaeologists have found that as early as 1400 B.C., dancing played an important part in religious ceremonies. A Cretan sword dance that is still performed today was described in *The Iliad*. Each Greek ceremony or event continues to be punctuated by a dance, whether solemn or festive.

To the Greeks, dancing is not only an artistic form of self-expression but also a release for bottled-up emotions. If a Greek hears bad news, he or she may stand up and start dancing alone. This does not mean the person is celebrating; he or she may be dancing to relieve the sorrow or the stress.

Greek folk dances are usually performed by a group of people, either arm-in-arm in a line or in an open circle moving counter-clockwise. The leader of the group often improvises, while the others follow the basic steps. There are hundreds of Greek dances and they all have different names, although they are often variations of one another. The *tavérna*, a casual restaurant, is a good place to see creative, invigorating dances.

THE FOLK DANCES OF GREECE

Folk dancing is an integral part of Greek culture. It is believed that the folk dances performed today originated in the ritual dances of ancient Greece. Every region in Greece has its own local folk dance; the costumes worn for each dance also vary according to the region.

The *zeibekiko* ("zay-BEK-kih-koh"), or "dance of the eagle," is commonly seen in *tavérnas*, and is danced alone or face-to-face with another person. Dancers hold out their arms like wings and slowly circle each other in a dance of combat. When one person performs a solo, the dancer moves around an imaginary partner. Often, the dancer seems to be in a trance. Spectators respect the privacy of the performer by not clapping, for the dance is meant to be performed only for the dancer and not for an audience.

The *syrtaki* ("sir-TAH-kee") is the most famous Greek dance. It is a mellow, expressive dance. The *syztaki* became internationally famous through the 1964 Hollywood movie *Zorba the Greek,* when it was danced by Anthony Quinn. Another popular dance is the *hasapiko* ("hah-SAH-pee-koh"), or butcher's dance. Several men dance slowly, holding each other's hands, and do the same steps in a solemn style.

The *tsamiko* ("SAH-mee-koh") is also called the "handkerchief dance" because the leader and the next dancer hold onto a handkerchief. The leader performs acrobatic stunts, using the handkerchief for support while the second dancer is holding it. This dance was widely performed by freedom fighters in the war for independence.

The *kalamatiano* ("kah-lah-mah-tee-ah-NOH") is the national dance of Greece. It is a happy, festive dance that originated in the Peloponnese but is now performed throughout the country; *kalamatiano* dancers stand in a row with their hands on each other's shoulders.

Greek youths enjoy a game of basketball, one of Greece's most popular sports.

SPORTS

Soccer, or *podosphéro* ("poh-DOHS-fay-roh"), is the most popular sport in Greece and the favorite topic of conversation among Greeks after politics. It is said the only time one finds the streets of Greece empty is during a televised Greek national soccer team match. Greece has a soccer league of 18 teams that play against one another on Sundays. Greeks are as devoted to this professional league as Americans are to major league baseball or professional football.

The second most popular sport is basketball. In 1987 Greece made its mark on the international scene by capturing the European basketball title. Since then, Greek basketball teams have won several major European trophies. As a result, the sport is becoming increasingly popular with young people and students of all ages.

Water sports are of great interest to the Greeks. Children learn to swim at a very early age because of Greece's proximity to the sea. Sailing, diving, and rowing regattas also draw many enthusiasts.

Automobile racing has gained much popularity in Greece over the last few decades. Thousands of spectators attend the Acropolis Rally each year, considered the toughest cross-country rally in the world.

HOME OF THE OLYMPIC GAMES

The ancient Greeks held Zeus, king of the gods, in great honor, and they built many temples for him, one of which was located at Olympia, in southwestern Greece. To pay tribute to him, they held athletic contests at Olympia every four years, laying the foundation for the Olympic Games.

The very first Olympic Games took place at Olympia around 776 B.C. Not only did the best athletes compete, but the finest artisans competed for distinction in their fields. The ideal man to the Greeks was one who could perform amazing physical feats as well as write poetry. The first recorded winner of a sports event was a cook named Coroebus, who finished first in a foot race.

Over the years, the Olympic Games became an important forum for the exchange of ideas among the leading citizens of Greece. The games became so much a part of national life that four-year periods were referred to as "olympiads" by the fourth century B.C. Peace reigned when the Olympic Games were held; all wars and quarrels were put aside.

As the number of events expanded, various structures were built to accommodate them—a hippodrome for chariot races, a gymnasium, and baths. Only male athletes competed, and in most events, the athletes competed in the nude. Women were not allowed to take part in the games or be in the audience. The only prizes awarded were olive wreaths.

In A.D. 393, the Roman emperor Theodosius I banned all pagan festivals and put an end to the games. Over 1,500 years later, the Olympic Games were once again brought to life.

In 1896, a Frenchman, Baron Pierre de Coubertin, revived the Olympic Games in Athens (*below*) after nine years of negotiations with the international community. Athletes from 13 countries competed. In the third modern Olympic Games, women were allowed to compete in archery, and by 1928, they were taking part in swimming and track events.

Greece is also home of the first marathon. After the battle of Marathon in 490 B.C., a runner was sent to Athens with news of the Greek victory. He ran the 26 miles (41.8 km) from Marathon to Athens and reported the news, then died of exhaustion. The race was created in his memory.

Athens will once again host the Olympic Games in 2004.

A scene from the 1998 film *Eternity and a Day* by Greek director Theo Angelopoulos.

MOVIES AND TELEVISION

Until the 1980s, Greece's broadcasting service was owned and regulated by the government. Many people complained that television programs lacked variety and news programs were often one-sided or incomplete. In 1991 the television industry was liberalized and opened to the private sector. Greece now has over 30 private television stations and about 20 satellite channels, plus cable and digital channels.

Going to the movies is a favorite pastime in Greece, and new movie complexes have been built in middle-class neighborhoods. They mostly show films from the United States, Britain, France, and Germany. Greek films are made on a limited budget, as they lack government subsidy. Still, several Greek films have been awarded prizes at international film festivals for their excellent content and cinematography. These films, however, appeal mostly to the avant-garde moviegoer and lack mass appeal.

THEATER

The summer season, from June through September, is an exciting time for theatrical events in Greece, which take place in open-air theaters.

One such event, the Athens Festival, has a program of concerts, dances, and ancient drama. Popular with Greeks and tourists, performances are held in the ancient Herodes Atticus Theater on the steps of the Acropolis. Another famous event is the Epidaurus Festival, devoted to the staging of tragedies and comedies written by ancient Athenian dramatists. The 14,000-seat arena dates back to the third century B.C.

The theater of Epidaurus is the best-preserved of all ancient theaters in Greece.

113

FESTIVALS

IN GREECE, FESTIVALS AND CELEBRATIONS are a part of everyday life. Many of these festivals have their roots in ancient traditions, but for the most part, festivals in Greece are connected with the Orthodox Church.

Since the Eastern Orthodox Church adopted the Gregorian calendar (introduced by Pope Gregory XIII in 1582 and now used by most of the world) in the 1920s, most Christian holidays in Greece fall at the same time of the year as they do in the rest of the world.

The exceptions to this are the holidays of Easter and Whitsun (a feast on the seventh Sunday after Easter), which are held according to the old Julian calendar, which was based on the phases of the moon.

Opposite: **Greek children fly their kites on "Clean Monday" at Filopapou Hill, next to the Acropolis. The day marks the end of the carnival season and the beginning of Lent, the 40-day fasting period leading to Easter.**

CALENDAR OF FESTIVALS

January	New Year's Day/Feast of St. Basil
	Epiphany
March	Independence Day/
	Annunciation of the Virgin Mary
April/May	Easter
	Feast of St. George
May	Labor Day/Flower Festival
	Pentecost
	Anastenaria/Feasts of St.
	Constantine and St. Helen
August	Dormition of the Virgin Mary
October	St. Demetrios' Day
	Ochi Day
December	St. Nicholas' Day/Christmas

Greeks in traditional dress dance during a religious festival.

FESTIVALS OF PATRON SAINTS

Every village celebrates a festival in honor of its patron saint. This is the saint to whom the local church is dedicated and the saint to whom the villagers are most devoted. The patron saint of Corfu is St. Spyridon. St. George is the patron saint of shepherds, and St. Nicholas is the patron saint of sailors.

All village communities organize their own merrymaking during saints' festivals. The celebrations begin with a Mass, with many twinkling candles lighting up the church. After Mass, the congregation shares in a huge meal cooked by the church council, and then the singing and dancing begin. People will go on singing and dancing for hours. Church bells peal the whole day through to inform other villages of the festival.

CHRISTMAS

On Christmas Eve, especially in the villages, groups of children go from house to house singing carols. The celebration of Christmas in Greece does not have a gift-giving tradition. Families do, however, have a festive Christmas dinner to end a 25-day "little Lent" period.

Instead of Christmas trees, Greek homes traditionally had a replica of a fishing boat with Christmas decorations. The ship is a symbol of the economic importance of the sea to Greeks. A wooden cross wrapped with a sprig of basil is the symbol of Christmas in Greece, for the basil is thought to ward off the *kallikantzarakia* ("kahl-ee-kahn-tzah-RAH-kee-ah"), the mischievous trolls that are said to disturb the household during the 12 days from Christmas to Epiphany. They are believed to knock over chairs, put out fires, and cause minor accidents in the house. Basil-soaked water is sprinkled throughout the house to ward off these spirits.

ST. BASIL'S DAY

St. Basil's Day, which also falls on New Year's Day, is a time for parties, presents, and good luck charms. St. Basil is the patron saint of the poor and needy. Gifts are exchanged, and a special St. Basil's cake is served. A coin is baked in the cake to symbolize St. Basil's generosity. Whoever finds the coin is believed to have good luck in the coming year.

Traditionally, rural Greeks go visiting family and friends on this day, and they customarily take some sand or a stone to the home they are visiting. The presentation of the sand or stone is said to ensure a good crop in the coming year. These gifts are piled up in the house for eight days before being thrown away.

Traditionally, Christmas celebrations in Greece did not include decorating a Christmas tree. In recent years, however, Christmas trees have become popular ways of attracting crowds of people to street Christmas festivities organized by the local government.

Greek Orthodox priests perform the traditional ceremony of the blessing of the sea on January 6, near Piraeus.

EPIPHANY

Epiphany, on January 6, marks the culmination of the Christmas season. On the eve of Epiphany, priests go from house to house sprinkling holy water. In some communities, a procession of carolers follows the priest.

A very important event called the "Blessing of the Waters" takes place in all seaside villages and towns on Epiphany. The event is of great importance to Greek sailors, whose vessels have been idle for the 12 days from Christmas to Epiphany. The biggest blessing takes place at Piraeus—all vessels, large and small, are decorated, and a church procession makes its way to the harbor carrying a cross that is ceremonially thrown into the sea. This is the signal for church bells to ring, ships' horns to blow, and warships to fire their cannons. Young men dive into the water to retrieve the cross, and the person who emerges with it is presented with gifts. He also has the honor of carrying the cross throughout the village and keeping it for the rest of the year.

NAME DAYS

In Greece, people celebrate their name day rather than their birthday. Since most Greek children are named after a famous saint, their name day is the feast day of their patron saint. On June 29, during the feast of St. Peter and St. Paul, all men and boys named Peter or Paul will celebrate.

Men and women usually stay home from work on their name days, and parties are thrown for children and their friends. Adults also welcome friends to their home on their name days. A special church service is held for all the people celebrating their name day, and those honored give candy to their friends.

INDEPENDENCE DAY AND OCHI DAY

A parade of schoolboys marches down the streets of Ioannina on Ochi Day.

Independence Day commemorates the war of independence against Turkey. The war began on March 25, 1821, as an armed uprising. After nearly four centuries of Turkish rule, the Greeks won their freedom in 1829. Every year on March 25, the Greeks celebrate Independence Day with parades and a display of fireworks.

Ochi Day is celebrated on October 28. *Ochi* ("OH-hee") is the Greek word for "no." In 1940, when Benito Mussolini, the Italian fascist dictator, demanded that Italian troops be allowed to enter Greece, the Greek prime minister at the time replied with a single word—*ochi!* War broke out between Italy and Greece and, to everyone's amazement, the poorly armed Greeks defeated the Italian army. Although the Germans eventually overran Greece, beginning the German occupation during World War II, the Greeks still commemorate their successful resistance of Italian troops.

A procession walks the town's streets on Easter Sunday.

EASTER SEASON

Easter is the most important holiday in the calendar of the Greek Orthodox Church. It is celebrated according to the Julian calendar, and usually falls in April, but sometimes in early May. Easter is deeply rooted in the Greek heart and soul; many Greeks living in the cities return to their home village for the celebrations. The Greek word for Easter is *Pascha* ("PAHS-kah").

The Easter season begins with a carnival season three weeks before Lent. On the last night before Lent, people eat and revel throughout the night for the last time before beginning the 40-day fast that marks Lent. "Clean Monday" signifies the beginning of Lent and is a day of fasting. On this day, Greeks will eat only unleavened bread and, traditionally, will climb a mountain to fly a kite, a symbol of release. During Lent, many Greeks do not eat meat, dairy products, or olive oil, or drink wine.

On Good Friday, strict fasting is observed. Funeral services to mark the death of Christ are held in all churches. The next day, Holy Saturday, a Resurrection Mass is celebrated, and at midnight, the clergy and choir chant hymns in the streets. The priest hands out the holy flame by lighting worshipers' candles and exclaims *"Christos anesti"* ("Chris-TOHS ah-NES-

Since Byzantine times, Greek festivals have centered around the Christian calendar. Churches support and encourage the local arts by promoting folk dance performances.

teh"), meaning "Christ is risen." Parishioners respond with "*Alithos anesti*" ("Ah-lee-THOS ah-NES-teh"), meaning "Indeed, He has risen."

Everyone then goes home, carrying the candles and the holy flame, as this signifies bringing home the spirit of Easter. The family feasts on soup and cakes. Hard-boiled eggs that have been dyed red to symbolize Christ's blood are knocked together. The egg that outlasts the rest brings luck to its holder. Fireworks are set off, and the feasting goes on into the night. On Easter Sunday Greeks attend church services at dawn in their holiday finery, perform folk dances, feast on the traditional meal of roast lamb, and welcome the start of spring.

FOOD

EATING AND DRINKING IN GREECE are not just a means of satisfying one's hunger and thirst—meals are also social events. Food and drink provide a very pleasant occasion for talking, arguing, socializing, gossiping, and making business deals.

Greeks have a culinary tradition that stretches back 2,800 years. One of the world's first cookbooks was written by Hesiod, who lived in the seventh century B.C. Literature shows that the ancient Greeks enjoyed baked fish, roast lamb, and honey cakes and used many of the herbs and spices that are still used by modern Greek cooks.

Above: **A typical Greek salad of lettuce, tomatoes, onions, and feta cheese, with olive oil dressing.**

Opposite: **A street vendor sells donuts and bread in Crete.**

TRADITIONAL FOOD AND DRINK

Geography and climate are strong influences on the cuisine of Greece. Although Greece is located in Europe, its close proximity to the Middle East, in addition to the years of Turkish rule, have given Greek cuisine a distinct Middle Eastern touch. The Turks brought coffee to Greece, and the Persians introduced rice, yogurt, and many sweet desserts.

On the Greek mountains, herds of sheep and goats provide meat and dairy products. Although chicken and pork are eaten in Greece, lamb remains the favorite meat, and goat's milk is used as a beverage and to make *feta* ("FEH-tah") cheese. As Greece is surrounded by the sea, fish and seafood seasoned with local lemon juice and tangy oregano are very popular dishes. Seafood is more commonly served in towns and villages close to the sea.

Greeks enjoy vegetables, such as eggplant, tomatoes, and olives. Their favorite seasonings are olive oil, lemon juice, garlic, basil, and oregano.

The Greek marketplace is a crowded, noisy, lively place.

THE OPEN-AIR MARKET OF ATHENS

In the center of Athens, on Athena Street, there is a large market that has been thriving for decades and is representative of markets located in towns throughout Greece.

The fish market is often mentioned in Greek literary texts; the market opens early and is always filled with shoppers. The floor is strewn with sawdust to soak up the melting ice. The air is filled with the smell of fish, and fishmongers noisily try to draw buyers to their stalls.

The meat market nearby has rows of whole lambs, pigs, calves, and poultry hanging on hooks. Meat vendors call out the advantages of their fine meats and persuade passers-by to buy from them.

Next might be the cheese shop, where fragrant cheeses stand in huge piles, while the cheese seller cuts off chunks of cheese to weigh for customers and to hand out as sample tidbits to tempt passers-by. Soft and white *feta* cheese is the most famous type of Greek cheese. *Feta* has been around since Homeric times, and it is estimated that the average Greek consumes more than 26 pounds (12 kg) of feta cheese per year.

Other types of Greek cheeses are *mizithra* ("mee-ZITH-rah"), *kasseri* ("kah-SEH-ree"), *kefalotyri* ("keh-fah-loh-TEE-ree"), *graviera* ("grah-vee-EH-rah"), and *manouri* ("mah-NOO-ree"). Greek cheese ranges from unsalted and soft to hard, salty, and strong-tasting.

Among some of the vegetables that are piled high at stalls in the market are eggplant, tomatoes, green peppers, okra, and assorted greens.

Markets can be found in almost every town in Greece. In some small villages, vendors go from door to door selling groceries.

POPULAR GREEK DISHES

Greeks enjoy many tasty appetizers that are served before the main meal. One of the best known is *taramosalata* ("tah-rah-moh-sah-LAH-tah"), a dip made of fish roe. Another dip, *tzatziki* ("zaht-ZEE-kee"), is made from cucumbers and garlic mixed with yogurt. These dips are delicious with either bread or vegetables.

Favorite Greek soups include *avgolémono* ("ahv-goh-LEH-moh-noh"), a chicken broth with rice, egg, and lemon juice, and *psarósoupa* ("sah-ROO-soo-pah"), a fish broth.

Meat dishes such as *souvláki* ("soov-LAH-kee"), or kebabs, and *keftédes* ("kef-THEH-des"), or meatballs, are well known in the West. *Moussaká* ("moo-sah-KAH"), a ground meat, eggplant, and cream pie, is also found in Turkey. *Dolmádes* ("dol-MAH-thehs") are vine leaves stuffed with ground meat and rice. *Styphádo* ("sti-FAH-thoh") is a meat stew.

Greek seafood, such as shrimp, crayfish, lobster, octopus, and squid, is usually served with a simple lemon and olive oil sauce. Fish is usually fried or grilled.

RECIPE FOR AVGOLÉMONO (EGG AND LEMON SOUP)

8 cups strong, strained chicken broth
$1/2$ cup uncooked rice
4 eggs
Juice of 2 lemons

Bring broth to a boil and add rice. Cook until rice is tender, about 20 minutes.

Remove broth from heat. Before serving, beat the eggs until they are light and frothy. Add lemon juice to eggs and beat slowly. Dilute egg and lemon mixture with two cups of broth, beating constantly until well mixed.

Add diluted egg-lemon mixture to the rest of the soup, mixing constantly. Heat soup and bring almost to boiling point, but do not overboil, or the soup will curdle.

Serve immediately.

MEALTIMES

Breakfast, or *proeeno* ("pro-ee-NOH"), is a light meal, usually eaten as early as 7 A.M. Many people have only Greek coffee, which is a strong, thick mixture of fine ground coffee, water, and sometimes sugar, boiled together. This is sometimes accompanied by a roll with butter, honey, or jelly.

Lunch, or *mesimeriano* ("meh-see-meh-ree-ah-NOH"), is the main meal, and it is eaten at home at 2 or 3 P.M. Appetizers, meat or fish, salad, yogurt with honey, and fruit may be served at a typical midday meal. Wine, beer, and water are common drinks for lunch. In summer, the midday meal is often followed by an afternoon nap, during which schools and businesses close.

Dinner is *deipnon* ("THEEP-non") in Greek. It is usually eaten in the late evening, perhaps as late as 10 P.M. But most Greeks have appetizers or *mezedakia* ("meh-zeh-DHAH-kee-ah") in the early evening, before dinner. Many little dishes of olives, cheese, freshly baked bread, and little bits of grilled lamb or broiled fish are served as snacks.

Family dinners at home may consist of the lunch meal, which has been heated up, but sweets are usually served after the fruit course.

Greeks often go out for dinner to a local *tavérna*. Rather than looking at a menu to make their selections, customers are allowed to go right into the kitchen and select from what the chef is cooking.

Cheese and olives are eaten in almost every Greek meal.

TABLE MANNERS AND SOCIAL GRACES

Because hospitality is considered a basic aspect of Greek culture and a natural extension of the Hellenic personality, there are no hard rules of etiquette. As in every other culture, however, certain table manners are observed:

- It is considered normal for dinner guests to arrive a few minutes late.
- At a meal, the male guest of honor is seated to the right of the hostess, while female guests are seated to the right of the host.
- The oldest guest is served first.
- Bread is placed on the table; there are no bread and butter plates.
- Hands do not rest on the lap and wrists must be kept on the table. In informal company, the elbows can rest on the table.
- Guests must eat heartily to avoid offending the host.
- It is common for close friends or relatives to eat from one another's plates.
- One of the most important things that a guest can do is compliment the host and hostess on the appearance of their home. Greeks spend many hours preparing for guests and feel very disappointed if no mention is made of it.

GREEK COFFEE

Greeks drink a dark, rich, finely ground coffee called *kafe* ("kah-FEH") or *kafedaki* ("kah-feh-DHAH-kee"). This is traditionally brewed in a long-handled pot known as a *briki* ("BREE-kee").

Briki pots come in two, four, or six *demitasse* cup sizes. Greek coffee is not made in larger quantities because the foam at the top, which is supposed to bring good luck, will not be of the right consistency. The coffee is served black, moderately sweet, or very sweet, and with a glass of cold water. *Kafedaki* is sipped carefully to avoid disturbing the grounds that settle to the bottom of the cup. A favorite pastime is to leave a little of the grounds in the cup, invert it on the saucer, and let it dry. Fortune-tellers can then read the future from the pattern of the dried grounds.

YIASSAS

The national drink of Greece is *ouzo* ("OO-zoh"), a clear spirit distilled from the residue of grapes after wine is made. It looks as innocent as water but has a strong licorice flavor and can have a 50 percent alcohol content. It is usually drunk straight, although some people prefer to add an ice cube, which instantly turns the liquid milky white.

Retsina ("ret-SEE-nah"), a classic Greek wine, has a very tangy resin taste. Some people believe that the wine was

Above: **Eating and drinking with friends is an important part of Greek social life. Greeks seldom eat or drink alone.**

Opposite: **A family meal in Greece.**

originally stored in casks made of pine, which leaked resin. Others say that the resin was a preservative and Greeks just grew accustomed to the taste over the years. Many believe that the resin helps in the digestion of oily, rich foods.

Before the first sip of an alcoholic beverage, Greeks always clink their glasses against those of their friends and make a toast. Usually they say "*yiassas*" ("YAH-sahs"), a wish for good health.

129

CHICKEN KEBAB

This recipe makes 4 to 5 servings.

1 pound (500 g) boneless chicken breasts
3 medium-size eggplants
2 medium-size red or green peppers
1 tablespoon finely chopped parsley
1 tablespoon finely chopped anise
1 tablespoon oregano
5 tablespoons olive oil
3 tablespoons lemon juice

Wash the eggplants, cut into small bite-size pieces, and sprinkle with salt. Cut the chicken into bite-size chunks. Cut peppers in half, remove seeds, and chop into bite-size pieces. Put parsley, anise, oregano, 3 tablespoons of olive oil, and lemon juice in a bowl and stir in the eggplants. Add chicken and peppers and mix thoroughly. Put the chicken, peppers, and eggplant on skewers. Place the skewers on a grill and grill each side of the skewers for 5 to 6 minutes. Baste them with 1 tablespoon of oil and lemon sauce once or twice. Finally, place the kebabs on a platter and serve with a green salad.

SPINACH PIE

Filling:
7 tablespoons olive oil
5–6 finely chopped medium-size onions
2.2 pounds (1 kg) spinach
5 eggs
1 cup finely chopped feta cheese
1 cup finely chopped gruyere cheese
1 cup milk

2 tablespoons finely chopped anise
Salt and pepper to taste

Piecrust:
$^3/_4$ cup olive oil
1 egg yolk
5 cups flour
Pinch of salt

Heat some olive oil in a large-size saucepan on medium heat. Add onions and fry for 2 to 3 minutes. Wash spinach and chop into large pieces. Put the spinach in the pot and stir. Let the mixture cook over low heat for 8 to 10 minutes. Remove the saucepan from the stove. Add eggs, feta, gruyere, milk, anise, salt, and pepper. Stir well. To make the piecrust, mix olive oil, egg yolk, flour, and salt in a bowl. Knead the dough, adding milk or water until the base becomes soft. Divide dough into two. Spread half of the dough out in a baking pan. Add spinach mixture over the base. Roll out other half of the dough evenly and cover the pie. Bake the pie in a 375°F (200°C) oven for 35 to 40 minutes until golden brown.

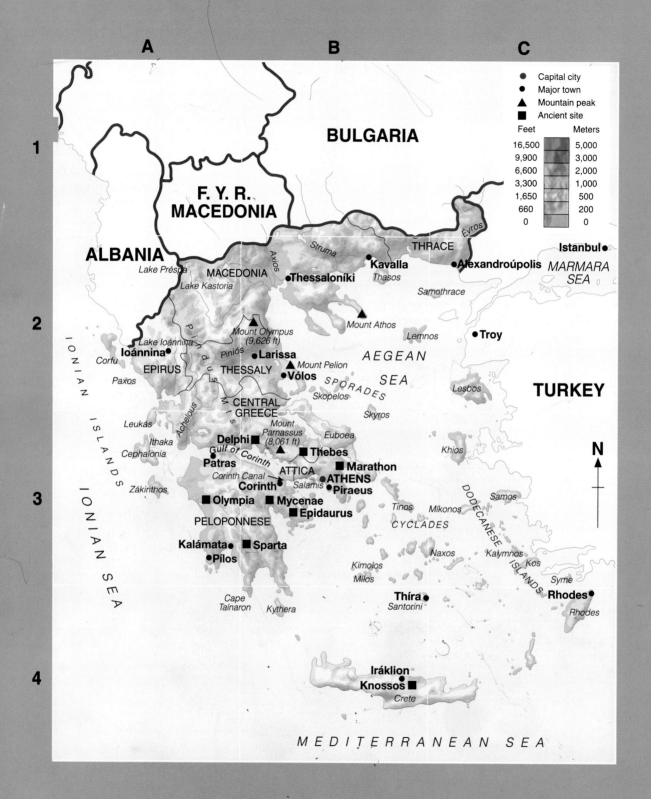

MAP OF GREECE

ECONOMIC GREECE

Agriculture

 Apples

 Olives

 Ouzo

 Tobacco

 Wine

Services

 Airport

 Port

 Tourism

Manufacturing

 Cement

 Fish products

ABOUT
THE ECONOMY

OVERVIEW

Greece's economy is one of the least developed in the EU and has benefited from financial aid and free trade with its EU partners. Agriculture in Greece, although the dominant sector until the 1950s, is expected to decrease in economic importance. Boasting a rich cultural heritage and idyllic beaches, tourism remains one of Greece's most important sectors, with potential for growth. Shipping, traditionally a strong economic sector, continues to be an energetic and expanding industry in Greece. Manufacturing of textiles and telecommunication equipment has also increased in the last few years.

GROSS DOMESTIC PRODUCT (GDP)

US$120 billion (2001)

ECONOMIC GROWTH RATE

3.5 percent (2001)

GDP PER CAPITA

US$11,350 (2001)

CURRENCY

The euro (EUR) replaced the Greek drachmae (GRD) in 2002 at a fixed rate of 340.750 drachmae per euro.
1 euro = 100 cents
USD 1 = EUR 1.03 (August 2002)
Notes: 5, 10, 20, 50, 100, 200, 500 euros
Coins: 1, 2, 5, 10, 20, 50 cents; 1, 2 euros

GDP SECTORS

Agriculture 8 percent, manufacturing 22 percent, services 70 percent (2001)

AGRICULTURAL PRODUCTS

Cotton, tobacco, olives, grapes, raisins, oranges, peaches, sugar, beets, wheat, corn, tomatoes

INDUSTRIES

Tourism, shipping, food and tobacco processing, textiles, chemicals, metal products, mining, petroleum products, cement

MAIN EXPORTS

Minerals (bauxite, magnesite, marble, lignite, lignite coal, and petroleum), fruit and vegetables, olive oil, textiles, clothing, wine

MAIN IMPORTS

Machinery, cars, trucks and buses, food, chemical products, petroleum and petroleum derivatives

MAIN TRADE PARTNERS

France, Germany, Italy, Japan, the Netherlands, the United Kingdom, the United States

TOURIST ARRIVALS

12 million (2001)

LABOR FORCE

4.5 million (1998). Services 59 percent, agriculture 20 percent, manufacturing 21 percent (2000)

UNEMPLOYMENT RATE

11 percent (2001)

CULTURAL GREECE

Pelion winter sports
Pelion Mountain was thought to be the summer residence of the Olympian gods; the town is a popular ski resort.

Thessaloníki Film Festival
The annual festival, held at one of Europe's cultural capitals, is a showcase for the work of young, emerging filmmakers in the Balkan region.

Anastenaria
This firewalking festival takes place in May on the feast day of St. Constantine and St. Helen, in Aghia Eleni, a town in northern Macedonia.

Mount Athos monasteries
Called the Holy Mountain, Athos is where 1,500 Greek Orthodox monks lead a communal life of seclusion in a complex of 20 monasteries. The first monastery was founded in A.D. 963

Patras Carnival
Highlights of the carnival, which dates back to the 1820s, are the parade of "black dominoes," women wearing a black cloak with a hood and a mask, and the treasure hunt.

The Cyclades summer sports
The islands of the Cyclades, such as Míkonos and Santorini, offer opportunities for rafting and canoeing, in addition to swimming and snorkeling in sparkling blue waters and sunny climate.

Epidaurus Festival
The world-famous festival is held every year from July to September at the 14,000-seat ancient theater at Epidaurus, built in the third century B.C. The festival celebrates Greece's classical tradition with performances of ancient Greek drama.

Kalámata Dance Festival
Since 1995, the city of Kalámata has hosted an annual dance festival in the month of July. The festival hosts world-renowned performers from around the world as well as local dance companies.

Acropolis
Complex of ancient buildings commissioned by Pericles, of which the most famous is the Parthenon, a temple dedicated to the goddess Athena, mythological founder of Athens, and completed in 432 B.C.

Athens Festival
Ancient Greek drama, music, and dance performances are held every year from June to September at the open-air theater Odeon of Herodes Atticus. Located at the Acropolis in Athens, the 5,000-seat theater was built in A.D. 161.

Crete wine festivals
In July, the villages of Rethymnon and Iráklion in Crete hold lively wine festivals, which include music, dance, and wine tasting.

Tinos Island's icon of the Virgin Mary
Thousands of Greek pilgrims crowd the quiet town of Tinos to pay their respects and seek physical healing from the icon of the Our Lady of Good Tidings, found during excavations prompted by a vision in 1822.

ABOUT THE CULTURE

OFFICIAL NAME
Hellenic Republic

NATIONAL FLAG
Nine horizontal blue and white stripes with a white cross in the upper left-hand corner. Blue and white represent the sea and the mountains of Greece. The cross symbolizes the Greek Orthodox Church.

NATIONAL ANTHEM
Hymn to freedom, a poem by Dionysios Solomos, describes the revolution against Turkish occupation.

CAPITAL
Athens

GEOGRAPHICAL REGIONS
Attica, Central Greece, Central Macedonia, Crete, Eastern Macedonia and Thrace, Epirus, Ionian islands, Northern Aegean, Peloponnese, Southern Aegean, Thessaly, Western Greece, Western Macedonia

OTHER MAJOR CITIES
Thessaloníki, Patras, Piraeus, Larissa

POPULATION
10.6 million (2001)

LIFE EXPECTANCY
76 years for men, 81 years for women (2001)

POPULATION GROWTH RATE
0.21 percent (2001)

ETHNIC GROUPS
Greek 98 percent; Albanian, Turk, Slav, and other 2 percent

RELIGIOUS GROUPS
Greek Orthodox 98 percent, Muslim 1.3 percent, other 0.7 percent

OFFICIAL LANGUAGE
Greek

LITERACY RATE
95 percent (2001)

NATIONAL HOLIDAYS
New Year's Day/St. Basil's Day (January 1), Independence Day (March 25), Easter (April or May), Labor Day (May 1), Whitsun (50 days after Easter), Ascension of the Virgin Mary (August 15), Ochi Day (October 28), Christmas (December 25)

LEADERS IN POLITICS
Konstantinos Karamanlis—first democratic leader (1974) after the junta
Andreas Papandreou—socialist leader (1981–89)
Constantine Simitis—prime minister since 1996

LEADERS IN THE ARTS
Theodoros Angelopoulos (filmmaker), Maria Callas (opera singer), Manos Chatzidakis (composer), Nikos Kazantzakis (writer), Mikis Theodorakis (songwriter),

TIME LINE

IN GREECE	IN THE WORLD
3000–1200 B.C. Cycladic, Minoan, and Mycenaean civilizations flourish.	
800–500 B.C. Archaic period; city-states rise.	**753 B.C.** Rome is founded.
500–336 B.C. Classical period; Golden Age of Athens (500–430 B.C.)	
431–404 B.C. Peloponnesian Wars	
350–205 B.C. Hellenistic period, under Macedonia	
146 B.C. Beginning of Roman rule	**116–17 B.C.** The Roman Empire reaches its greatest extent, under Emperor Trajan (98–17).
A.D. 395 Byzantine empire begins.	**A.D. 600** Height of Mayan civilization
	1000 The Chinese perfect gunpowder and begin to use it in warfare.
1204 Invasion by crusader armies of Venetians, Franks, and others	**1530** Beginning of trans-Atlantic slave trade organized by the Portuguese in Africa.
1453 Constantinople, capital of the Byzantine empire, falls to Ottoman Turks. Turkish domination begins.	**1558–1603** Reign of Elizabeth I of England
	1620 Pilgrim Fathers sail the *Mayflower* to America.
	1776 U.S. Declaration of Independence
	1789–99 French Revolution
1821–29 War of independence; Turkish sultan recognizes Greek independence.	
1832 Britain, France, and Russia place Otto of Bavaria as king of Greece.	

IN GREECE	IN THE WORLD
1863	**1861**
Danish prince William is crowned King George I of Greece.	U.S. Civil War begins.
1908	**1869**
Crete joins Greece.	The Suez Canal is opened.
1912–13	
Balkan Wars. The remaining regions of modern-day Greece are liberated from Turkish rule.	
1914–18	**1914**
Greece sides with Allies in World War I.	World War I begins.
1922	
Greece is defeated by Turks in Asia Minor. Brutal population exchange of Turks and Greeks between both countries.	
1936–40	**1939**
Military dictatorship of Ioánnis Metaxas	World War II begins.
1940	
Metaxas denies Mussolini's troops entry and Greeks drive out Italian army.	
1941–45	**1945**
Nazi occupation	The United States drops atomic bombs on Hiroshima and Nagasaki.
	1949
	North Atlantic Treaty Organization (NATO) is formed.
1967–74	**1957**
Military dictatorship by "the Colonels"	Russians launch Sputnik.
1975	
Parliament abolishes monarchy.	
1981	
Greece joins the European Community. Andreas Papandreou's socialist party (PASOK) wins elections.	**1991**
	Break-up of the Soviet Union
	1997
	Hong Kong is returned to China.
2002	**2001**
Greece adopts the euro.	World population surpasses 6 billion.

GLOSSARY

authoritative regime
A dictatorship; a government that is centered on one powerful figure or a small group of leaders not elected by the people.

bora
A strong, cold wind that originates in the Balkan mountains and blows to Greece from the north or northeast.

bouzoúki ("boo-ZOO-kee")
A banjo-like instrument that accompanies folk songs.

chimera
A monster in Greek mythology, usually represented as having a lion's head, a goat's body, and a serpent's tail.

democracy
A system of government that originated in the Greek city-states, in which the leaders are chosen by the people they govern.

dimotiki ("dee-moh-tee-KEE")
Demotic Greek, the common language of Greece.

kafeneíon ("kah-fay-NEE-on")
A Greek café.

katharévousa ("kah-thah-REH-voo-sah")
An artificial language based on ancient Greek that was the official language of Greece from the 1830s to 1976.

kéfi ("KEH-fee")
A feeling of joy and celebration.

komboloi ("kohm-boh-LOY")
Worry beads used to help relieve stress.

koumbaros ("koom-BAH-rohs")
A godparent or spiritual member of the family.

infrastructure
The basic public facilities serving a country, such as roads, transportation and communication systems, and power plants.

mythology
A collection of stories about the creation of the world and the lives of gods and goddesses.

ouzo ("OO-zoh")
The national drink of Greece; a clear spirit distilled from the residue of grapes after wine is made.

philotimo ("feel-LOH-tee-moh")
A tradition of gaining respect from others by upholding one's and one's family's honor.

philoxenia ("feel-lox-eh-NEE-ah")
The Greek tradition of hospitality.

polis ("POH-lis")
A city-state in ancient Greece.

yiassas ("YAH-sahs")
Cheers or a toast to health.

FURTHER INFORMATION

BOOKS

Biers, William R. *The Archaeology of Greece: An Introduction*. Ithaca: Cornell University Press, 1996.
Boardman, John. *Greek Art*. London, United Kingdom: Thames & Hudson, 1996.
Homer, Robert Fagles (Translator). *The Iliad/the Odyssey*. New York City: Penguin USA, 1999.
Jones, Jayne Clard. *The Greeks in America*. Minneapolis: Lerner Publications Company, 1992.
Nardo, Don. *Modern Nations of the World: Greece*. San Diego: Lucent Books, 2000.
Nardo, Don. *Readings on Sophocles*. San Diego: Greenhaven Press, 1997.
Rawlins, Clive L. *Culture Shock!: Greece*. Portland: Graphic Arts Center Publishing Company, 2001.
Yeoh, Hong-Nam. *Countries of the World: Greece*. Milwaukee: Gareth Stevens Publishing, 1999.

WEBSITES

Ancient Greece, information on art, architecture, literature, geography, history. www.ancientgreece.com
Embassy of Greece in Washington, D.C. www.greekembassy.org
Greek food recipes. www.mealsforyou.com/cgi-bin/search (enter "Greek")
Greek language. www.greece.org/gr-lessons/gr-english/
Greek National Tourism Organization. www.greektourism.gr
Official site of Athens 2004 Olympic Games. www.athens2004.gr
Online magazine on contemporary Greece, including country profile, news, and Greek language. www.greece.gr
Parthenon marbles. www.damon.gr/marbles
Lonely Planet World Guide: Destination Greece. www.lonelyplanet.com/destinations/europe/greece
University of Pennsylvania Museum of Archaeology and Anthropology: The Ancient Greek World. www.museum.upenn.edu/Greek_World/index.html

MUSIC

All the Best from Greece. Montreal, Canada: Madacy Records, 1994.
Mouskouri, Nana. *Athina*. Santa Monica: Universal/Polygram, 1997.
Mondo Greece. Sherman Oaks: Ark 21 Records, 2002.
Royal Greek Festival Company. *Authentic Greek Folk Songs and Dances*. Sharon: Folk-Legacy Records, Inc., 1994.

VIDEOS

Discovering Greece (*Video Visits Travel Collection*). New Hope: Questar, Inc., 2001.
Z. Los Angeles: Fox Lorber, 1969.

BIBLIOGRAPHY

Ardley, Bridget. *Greece*. Englewood Cliffs: Silver Burdett, 1989.

Arnold, Frances. *Greece*. Austin: Steck-Vaughn, 1992.

Fisher, John and Marc Dubin. *The Rough Guide to Greece*. London, United Kingdom: Rough Guides, 2000.

Greece in Pictures. Minneapolis: Lerner Publications Company, 1992.

Katsadorakis, George. *The Natural Heritage of Greece*. Athens, 2000.

Kebric, Robert B. *Greek People*. Mountain View: Mayfield Publications Company, 1989.

Kochilas, Diane. *The Glorious Foods of Greece: Traditional Recipes from Islands, Cities and Villages*. New York: William Morrow & Co., 2001.

Lawrence, A. W. and R. A. Tomlinson. *Greek Architecture*. New Haven: Yale University Press, 1996.

Microsoft Encarta Encyclopedia 2000.

Powell, Anton. *Ancient Greece*. New York: Facts on File, 1989.

Willett, David et. al. *Lonely Planet: Greece*. 5th edition. Hawthorn, Australia: Lonely Planet Publications, 2002.

Archelon—The Sea Turtle Protection Society of Greece. www.archelon.gr

Greek National Tourism Organization. www.greektourism.gr

Greenpeace Greece. www.greenpeace.gr

World Wide Fund For Nature Greece. www.wwf.gr

INDEX